Our Rights, Our Future

Human Rights Based Approaches in Ireland: Principles, Policies and Practice

international
human rights
network

Acronyms

CAT	Convention Against Torture
CEDAW	Convention on the Elimination of All Forms of Discrimination against Women
CERD	Convention on the Elimination of All Forms of Racial Discrimination
CRC	Convention on the Rights of the Child
CRG	Constitution Review Group
CIDA	Canadian International Development Agency
CCA	Common Country Assessment (UN)
CORI	Conference of Religious in Ireland
DANIDA	Danish International Development Agency
DFID UK	Department for International Development
ECHR	European Convention on Human Rights and Fundamental Freedoms
ESC	Economic, Social and Cultural (rights)
EU	European Union
HRBA	Human Rights Based Approaches
HURIST	Human Rights Strengthening Programme (UN)
ICCPR	International Covenant on Civil and Political Rights
ICESCR	International Covenant on Economic, Social and Cultural Rights
ILO	International Labour Organisation
IMF	International Monetary Fund
MDGs	Millennium Development Goals
NAPS	National Anti-Poverty Strategy
NGO	Non-Governmental Organisation
NHRAP	National Human Rights Action Plan
NORAD	Norwegian Agency for Development
OECD	Organization for Economic Cooperation and Development
ODI	Overseas Development Institute
OHCHR	Office of the United Nations High Commissioner for Human Rights
PRSP	Poverty Reduction Strategy Paper
SIDA	Swedish International Development Agency
TD	Teachta Dála (member of Dáil Éireann)
UDHR	Universal Declaration of Human Rights
UNDAF	United Nations Development Assistance Framework
UNHCR	United Nations High Commissioner for Refugees
UNICEF	United Nations Children's Fund
UNIFEM	United Nations Development Fund for Women
UNDP	United Nations Development Programme
WHO	World Health Organization
WTO	World Trade Organization

Table of Contents

Preface

"All human beings are born free and equal in dignity and rights."
Article 1 of the Universal Declaration of Human Rights

"To deny any person their human rights is to challenge their very humanity."
Nelson Mandela

Human rights are inherent to each and every one of us. They are set out in international human rights law, and states are legally bound to promote, protect and fulfil them. They span all areas of life: civil activity, political freedom, social needs, economic well-being, cultural pursuits and environmental quality.

The human rights framework is a relatively new global development. Emerging from the horrors of World War II, the international community agreed the UN Charter (1946), and the Universal Declaration of Human Rights (1948). All international human rights law developed from this starting point.

Over the decades, governments, communities and organizations have come to understand that human rights are not just ends or goals to which we vaguely aspire. Nor are they some perfect utopia that we can all dream about. They are the benchmarks of a just society. Moreover, they provide the means to deliver real justice and equality. In essence, they give people the right to have control over their lives and future.

The challenge is clear – how do we use the human rights framework to make life better for everyone? Human rights are not just laws: they shape a process and provide a series of approaches that can show governments and society how to build a fairer, more equitable society.

This thinking led to the emergence of human rights based approaches to development, i.e. the understanding that human development improves when we use human rights as the framework. Put another way, we know now that charity and chequebooks are not enough. Real change involves changing attitudes and deepening understanding. For that to come about, we have to engage in partnerships and participation. While human rights are the entitlement of everyone on an equal basis, the level of development of a society can be measured by the extent to which we include and protect the most marginalised and most vulnerable; by our standards of accountability; by the extent to which people are empowered.

Human rights based approaches are now used increasingly in the developing world - but they are equally essential as the ideal framework for governance in all countries, including here in Ireland. Democracy and human rights are inseparable. What is required in Ireland is a system that is uncontaminated by prejudice and divorced from clientelism. When Irish Government ministers ignore the views of the state's own human rights advisory bodies, what they are demonstrating is fear of the accountability, transparency and rigour of international law. Many groups representing, for example, the elderly, children, educators, people with a disability, women, unmarried fathers, marginalised groups such as Travellers, the homeless, refugees, etc. have accurately identified human rights based approaches as the way forward to address their needs and deliver on their entitlements.

Amnesty International members, working worldwide since 1961, have direct experience of situations where human rights have created the climate that has allowed societies to rise out of poverty, to build democracy, to improve healthcare systems, and to provide education and housing. It continues to astound and frustrate Amnesty when we see governments undermining human rights when we know that they provide the solutions for human security in the true meaning of the term – freedom from want, freedom from fear, and freedom to act on one's own behalf.

Informed by this understanding, Amnesty International (Irish Section) commissioned the International Human Rights Network to provide a framework document that would outline the internationally agreed core minimum principles for human rights based approaches, and examine them in an Irish context. We anticipate that this document will be of use as a reference point for government, non-governmental organisations (NGOs), community groups, and individuals seeking to address inequalities, discrimination, and injustice in our society.

This framework document is just one element of a larger initiative Amnesty is stewarding that seeks to build the capacity of interested individuals and organisations to use human rights based approaches in Ireland. This document will be the basis for further publications, including a campaigning tool-kit and more in-depth papers focusing on specific sectors or issues. The project also includes training, mentoring, research, conferences and the provision of a web-based resource point on human rights based approaches.

Colm Ó Cuanacháin
Secretary General, Amnesty International (Irish Section)

PART ONE:

HUMAN RIGHTS BASED APPROACHES

1. Introduction

This document aims to provide a basic framework for understanding and promoting human rights based approaches in Ireland today. It is designed to assist civil society in influencing key policy-makers and opinion-formers so as to ensure that national policies, law reform and practices are based on human rights.

The document applies the human rights framework to the development choices Ireland has made in recent years, incorporating feedback from a range of organisations and individuals.[1] Illustrations are drawn from typical experiences of individuals and groups in Ireland.

We hope this document will serve as a campaigning tool, and that it will inform activities and training programmes on human rights based approaches. A list of useful materials is contained in the resource bibliography in Annex 1 at the end of the document. A glossary is provided in Annex 2, to explain the various bodies to which reference is made.

Part One of the document provides a conceptual framework of human rights based approaches (HRBA), including the historical international evolution of the concept to date and the 'core minimum' considerations which need to inform HRBA in Ireland.

Part Two explores Ireland's experience applying human rights based approaches to its development to date. The practical consequences arising from the core concepts underlying HRBA are explored through illustrations drawn from typical profiles of individuals and groups. The overview of the current situation and the illustrations both serve to highlight current levels of understanding of human rights based approaches and key challenges faced. The document concludes with recommendations aimed at HRBA.

The preparation of this framework document involved a review of recent developments regarding HRBA on the international level, as well as an exploration of current policy and practice in Ireland. This involved analysis of primary written materials, interviews and small group discussions as well as feedback on discussion drafts. In addition, the document was shared by Amnesty with partner organisations and individuals that are part of its wider Human Rights Based Approaches Initiative. In Annex 3 are three NGO responses to questionnaires about their HRBA work.

> "In each situation we confront, a rights-based approach requires us to ask: *What* is the content of the right? *Who* are the human rights *claim-holders*? *Who* are the corresponding *duty-bearers*? Are claim-holders and duty-bearers *able to claim their rights and fulfil their responsibilities*? If not, *how can we help them* to do so? This is the heart of a human rights-based approach."
>
> **Mary Robinson, former UN High Commissioner for Human Rights, comments at 2nd Interagency Workshop on Implementing a Rights-based Approach in the Context of UN Reform, May 2003.**

Endnote

1. The document incorporates feedback received on the discussion draft from a range of organizations and individuals on the basis of non-attribution during May-July 2005.

"[T]he peoples of the United Nations have in the Charter reaffirmed their faith in fundamental human rights, in the dignity and worth of the human person and in the equal rights of men and women **and have determined to promote social progress and better standards of life in larger freedom...**"

Preamble, Universal Declaration of Human Rights, 1948

2. The principles of human rights based approaches

I t is important to be clear as to the definitions and concepts used here. This chapter outlines the core meaning of the terms "human rights", "development" and "human rights based approaches" (referred to as HRBA).

2.1 Human rights defined

The term human rights is used throughout as encompassing the full spectrum of internationally recognised human rights - civil, cultural, economic, political and social.

The 1948 Universal Declaration of Human Rights (UDHR) is the first international written declaration of the basic human rights of all mankind, and was drafted by the United Nations (UN) in the aftermath of World War II. The ambition behind it was to create a world where the dignity and humanity of each and every person would be respected by all nations. The binding conventions subsequently adopted by the UN and ratified by states provide a valuable degree of accountability in how states treat their populations today. (See box: "What is a Convention?")

There are two main sources of binding international human rights law: customary international law and conventions (also called treaties). Customary international law is made up of principles so widely accepted by nations as binding even where they are not written legal standards. The concept that a government must provide asylum from persecution (called *non-refoulement*), for instance, is a norm of customary international law, so that, even if a State has not ratified, or decides to withdraw from, the 1951 UN Convention relating to the Status of Refugees, the obligation is binding nonetheless. Also, over time, what might have begun as a "soft law" principle[2] (i.e. a non-binding standard) may become so widely accepted that it "hardens" into binding international "hard law". The UDHR, adopted in 1948 as a non-binding UN General Assembly Resolution, is an example of a soft law that is now widely considered to have become binding customary international law.

Eleanor Roosevelt holding a copy of the Universal Declaration of Human Rights, drafted and approved by the UN Human Rights Commission under her chairmanship.
© UN Photo

While the categorisation of human rights has been the subject of international debate influenced by cold war politics, the UDHR, the foundation of 20th century human rights law, makes no distinction between different human rights. All international human rights treaties to which Ireland is party, from the International Covenant on Civil and Political Rights to the International Covenant on Economic, Social and Cultural Rights, have equal legal status as binding treaties.

The equal status of all human rights was reaffirmed in 1993, when 170 states, including Ireland, reached consensus at the World Conference on Human Rights in Vienna.[3] The Vienna Declaration and Programme of Action[4] re-stated the legal principles that all internationally recognised human rights are universal, inalienable, interrelated and interdependent. The universality of human rights means that they are to be enjoyed by everyone, without discrimination, throughout the world. Their inalienability means that they are inherent in each

What is a convention?

A **convention** (also called a treaty) is a legally binding contract between nations. When a state ratifies a convention, it is called a "State Party" to that convention.

The convention that established the framework for the United Nations, the **1945 UN Charter**, commits Member States to promote universal respect for human rights. Article 103 of the UN Charter establishes that: "In the event of a conflict between the obligations of the Members of the United Nations under the present Charter and their obligations under any other international agreement, their obligations under the present Charter shall prevail."

The major UN human rights conventions have **treaty-based oversight committees** which issue guidelines on the interpretation of the conventions, known as **"General Comments"**. States Parties to these conventions agree to report periodically to these committees on the steps that they have taken to implement the provisions of the conventions. Nongovernmental organizations can also submit information for review by a committee when it is assessing a State's compliance – these NGO reports are called **"Shadow Reports"**. The committee then issues conclusions and recommendations to the Government of the State.

In some countries, international law is automatically part of national law, and enforceable in their national courts – a legal system called "monism". In Ireland, and most countries, however, domestic legislation must be enacted to **"incorporate"** international law – this system is called "dualism" – and while this is usually a stated obligation when a treaty is ratified, it is not always complied with. There is also a difference between **signing** and **ratifying** a convention. Signing indicates an intention to ratify, whereas ratifying means that the State is thereby legally bound by the convention's provisions.

Some conventions, such as the International Covenant on Civil and Political Rights, have **individual complaints mechanisms** (usually provided in a separate Optional Protocol which the State must also ratify), whereby individuals may directly request an oversight committee to investigate an allegation that their rights have been violated by the State Party.

The **International Bill of Rights** is comprised of two conventions adopted in 1966: the **International Covenant on Economic, Social and Cultural Rights** (ICESCR) and the **International Covenant on Civil and Political Rights** (ICCPR). While the division of rights between these two conventions is artificial, the fact that the rights contained in the UDHR were spilt into two conventions was due to the global ideological divide during the Cold War when they were drafted.

There are two different types of enforcement requirements for the rights contained in these two conventions. The two types of obligations can be described as an **"obligation of result"** and an **"obligation of conduct"**. Article 2(1) of the ICCPR requires governments to "respect and ensure" the enforcement of **civil and political rights**. This has been called an "obligation of result" because it requires governments not only to "respect" rights as a matter of law, but also to "give effect" to these rights, i.e. to "ensure" their enforcement. Since they are more likely to require government planning and the investment of resources, the ICESCR creates a requirement of **"progressive realization"** of **economic, social and cultural rights**. The ICESCR imposes immediate obligations on governments to "to take steps" (i.e. begin planning) to bring about the full enjoyment of the rights contained in the ICESCR, and "particularly the adoption of legislative measures". While the ICESCR has been described as establishing an "obligation of conduct" (i.e. to take action) rather than an "obligation of result", the ICESCR also creates immediate obligations on States Parties to the convention. For example, the principle of non-discrimination has immediate effect.

The other five of the seven major UN human rights conventions contain a mixture of economic, social, cultural, civil and political rights.

individual, not a gift or privilege given by authorities and they cannot be taken away. The principle that human rights are interdependent and inter-related recognises that the full enjoyment of any particular human right depends upon the enjoyment of others. For example, the enjoyment of the right to health is dependent on the right to housing5 and the right to education (e.g. regarding diet/lifestyle, transmission of HIV/Aids). Similarly, the exercise of the right to vote is dependent on the vindication of the right to housing. The right to equality underscores all of these rights.

Under human rights law, the State has primary responsibility to **respect**, **protect** and **fulfil** the human rights of all those in its territory. To respect human rights means the State has a duty not to interfere directly or indirectly with their enjoyment. Protecting human rights means the State must proactively provide a system which prevents, protects from, and provides redress for, interference by individuals or bodies not working for the State ("non-state actors"),[6] such as neighbours, spouses or companies.[7] The State obligation's to fulfill human rights requires it to ensure that they are fully enjoyed, whether through adopting appropriate legislative, administrative, budgetary, judicial or other measures.

Modern international human rights law is the product of a consensus reached by states as to the *minimum standards they agree to be bound by*, e.g. in the right to education and the right to health. The methods by which those standards are met are a matter of discretion for each state. For example, while the standards required to comply with the right to fair trial are clear and detailed (right to a defence, presumption of innocence, etc.), a wide variety of types of legal system (Civil Law, Common Law, etc.) meet those standards throughout the world. Moreover, international human rights is an evolving body of law, as reflected in moves to make non-state actors accountable and to develop rights based approaches to new issues such as the environment.

By its participation in the international human rights framework Ireland has undertaken to ensure that its Constitution, laws, policies, budgets and practices reflect these legal obligations and achieve, rather than undermine, the minimum standards to which it has agreed. This applies to all branches of the State and to all levels, including local authorities. Ireland, no less than the countries it supports through development aid, is legally obliged to ensure that its development plans (whether social, economic, etc.) are assessed in terms of their human rights impact before and during implementation. This obligation extends to regulating the behaviour of third parties involved in, or otherwise impacting on, development processes – e.g. corporations – to ensure that all human rights are effectively enjoyed in Ireland.

The debate regarding environmental protection is illustrative of the evolutionary nature of human rights law. Protection of the natural environment is fundamentally interconnected with the realization of a range of human rights. States are obliged to ensure, at the very least, that environmental degradation does not seriously impair the right to life, the right to the highest attainable standard of health, the right to an adequate standard of living, and in particular the right to safe and adequate food and clean water. The UN Committee on Economic, Social and Cultural Rights has stated that violations of the right to health include "the failure to enact or enforce laws to prevent the pollution of water, air and soil by extractive and manufacturing industries."[8] Environmental pollution has also been linked to the right to freedom of information (to enable those living near activities with the potential to cause environmental pollution to make informed decisions),[9] the right to participate in decision-making which may affect the realization of rights,[10] and the right to privacy.[11]

It is also the duty of the State to protect other states from harmful acts by private individuals or companies within its jurisdiction. According to Article 14 of the UN Human Rights Norms for Business, such non-state enterprises are responsible for the environmental and human health impact of their activities, and "shall take appropriate measures in their activities to reduce the risk of accidents and damage to the environment by adopting best management practices and technologies".[12] The Norms further provide: "on a periodic basis (preferably annually or biannually), transnational corporations and other business enterprises shall assess the impact of their activities on the environment and human health".

Reviewing progress on the 1992 United Nations Conference on Environment and Development (UNCED) in promoting and protecting human rights in relation to environmental questions, and in implementing Agenda 21,[13] the global plan of action on the environment agreed by member states and organizations of the UN, a UN-hosted meeting of experts on human rights and the environment concluded: "respect for human rights is broadly accepted as a pre-condition for sustainable development, ... environmental protection constitutes a pre-condition for the effective enjoyment of human rights protection, and ... human rights and the environment are interdependent and inter-related. These features are now broadly reflected in national and international practices and developments."[1]

> ### "Human Rights" are not limited to rights recognised under national law
>
> Human rights commitments undertaken in international treaties are recognised as inherent to the human being and cannot be undermined by a Constitution or other national law. In fact, by becoming a party to international treaties, the State is undertaking as a matter of law that its national arrangements (Constitution, laws, budgets, practices, etc.) comply with that standard. Where national law or practice falls short of human rights standards to which the state has agreed, the state violates its international legal obligations.
>
> So, in some cases, "rights" provided under national law fail to meet the standard required by international human rights law. On the other hand, a state can also choose to provide a higher standard of human rights protection than the minimum standard of behaviour set out on the international level.

2.2 Development defined

The 1986 Declaration on the Right to Development, adopted by the UN General Assembly, defines development as a comprehensive economic, social, cultural and political process.[15] Its object is the constant improvement of the well-being of the entire population and of all individuals, on the basis of their active, free and meaningful participation and it applies to all states, whether described as developing or not. The internationally agreed definition of development involves therefore, not just economic growth, or macroeconomic performance, but all areas of national life such as health, environment, housing, education, distribution of resources, enhancement of people's capabilities, and widening of their choices.

The emphasis on *process* as well as *outcomes* means that development is a composite of civil, political, economic, social and cultural human rights. It is rooted in the provisions of the Charter of the United Nations, the Universal Declaration of Human Rights, and the key

"The protection of the environment is... a vital part of contemporary human rights doctrine, for it is a sine qua non for numerous human rights such as the right to health and the right to life itself. It is scarcely necessary to elaborate on this, as damage to the environment can impair and undermine all the human rights spoken of in the Universal Declaration and other human rights instruments."

Judge Weeramantry, *Case Concerning the Gabcíkovo-Nagymaros Project* (Hungary v Slovakia), International Court of Justice in The Hague, 1997

Protesters highlight the connection between issues in Ireland and developing countries.
© *Indymedia*

international human rights treaties to which Ireland is a party, including the International Covenant on Civil and Political Rights, the International Covenant on Economic, Social and Cultural Rights and the Convention on the Rights of the Child. In 1993, the World Conference on Human Rights in Vienna, in which Ireland participated, affirmed by consensus the right to development.

International human rights law also underpins and supports the principle that development must also be sustainable, i.e. "development that meets the needs of the present without compromising the ability of future generations to meet their own needs".[16] In 2003, the UN Commission on Human Rights adopted a decision on "Human rights and the Environment as Part of Sustainable Development", reaffirming that "peace, security, stability and respect for human rights and fundamental freedoms, including the right to development, as well as respect for cultural diversity are essential for achieving sustainable development and ensuring that sustainable development benefits all, as set forth in the Plan of Implementation of the World Summit on Sustainable Development".[17]

2.3 Human rights based approaches

Human rights based approaches (HRBA) to development are processes which apply a number of core principles. Adherence to these core principles requires that the means and the results of all development seek to ensure the full enjoyment of human rights by all. It is important to emphasise that a range of human rights based approaches have been developed. Which approach is likely to be most effective varies according to the circumstances, such as the particular sector being addressed, the social and political context, and the different actors seeking to employ HRBA. HRBA are, however, united by a common purpose and core principles, even if different actors adopt different formulations.[19]

HRBA seek to ensure that human rights are a central frame of reference in policymaking and political choices by ensuring that people have the political, institutional and material means to demand, exercise and monitor their human rights, and to actively participate in decision-making processes. It has been described as the "scaffolding of development policy".[20] It entails more than formal commitment to respect human rights norms and standards. It requires the integration of those minimum standards into all plans, policies, budgets, processes and institutions. By definition HRBA is as concerned with the *process* as well as the *outcome*.

In the context of poverty reduction, for example, HRBA require not only that alleviation strategies and goals be explicitly based on the norms and values of international human rights law, but also that those strategies be identified, applied and reviewed with active and informed participation of the disadvantaged and marginalised. The use of human rights language and participatory processes empowers these groups to both assert their human rights and hold accountable those legally responsible for their delivery.

Former UN High Commissioner for Human Rights, Mary Robinson, has highlighted how HRBA leads to more effective, more sustainable, more rational development processes.[21] The five inter-connected principles, which have been internationally recognised as forming the core of HRBA (and which will be discussed in more depth in Part 2), are: 1. Express application of the international human rights framework; 2. Empowerment; 3. Participation; 4. Non-discrimination and prioritisation of vulnerable groups; and 5. Accountability.

The flags of the member states outside the United Nations Headquarters in New York.
© UN/DPI

Outlined in Table 1, these principles are themselves part of the legally binding framework applicable to Ireland, which is further explained in Part Two. The sources and content of each principle are outlined in Part Two. The principles are employed as the lens through which Ireland's ongoing economic, social, cultural and political progress – i.e. its development – must be evaluated.

"What is a rights-based approach to development?

A rights-based approach to development is a conceptual framework for the process of human development that is normatively based on international human rights standards and operationally directed to promoting and protecting human rights.

Essentially, a rights-based approach integrates the norms, standards and principles of the international human rights system into the plans, policies and processes of development. The norms and standards are those contained in the wealth of international treaties and declarations. The principles include equality and equity, accountability, empowerment and participation. A rights-based approach to development includes the following elements:

- express linkage to rights
- accountability
- empowerment
- participation
- non-discrimination and attention to vulnerable groups"

UN Office of the High Commissioner for Human Rights,
www.unhchr.ch/development/approaches-04.html

A human rights based approach (HRBA) is a process which applies a number of core principles aimed at ensuring the full enjoyment of human rights by all.

"It is the way we do business that has to change. This is not a matter simply of the introduction of new "human rights" projects or.... the infusion of human rights language, or by the addition of human rights components."

UN Human Rights Strengthening Programme, Review 2001

United Kingdom Prime Minister Atlee addresses the first meeting of the UN General Assembly, London on 10th January 1946
© *UN/DPI*

Table 1. Five core principles of HRBA[22]

HRBA Core Principles	Application in Practice
1. Expressly apply human rights framework	Define the goals of all development in terms of the relevant international human rights commitments of the state – as legally enforceable entitlements on the national level. This necessarily includes: - Explicitly taking human rights obligations into account at every stage of national and local development processes (from the identification of needs through to policy and programme identification as well as implementation, monitoring and evaluation). - Addressing the full spectrum of indivisible, interdependent and interrelated rights: civil, cultural, economic, political and social. - Ensuring that all sectors of national planning reflect the human rights framework (for example, health, education, housing, justice administration and political participation). - Building the capacity of public representatives, civil servants and local officials so that they apply the human rights framework in their work (e.g. through recruitment, training and specialised advice).
2. Empowerment	Ensure policies and programmes are based on empowerment - not "charity". This means ensuring people have the power, capacities (including education and information), as well as access needed to improve their own communities and influence their own lives. Ensure that rights holders and duty bearers share a common understanding of human rights goals and the duties to respect, protect, and fulfil them. This means systematically educating and raising awareness of Government, public representatives, civil servants, service providers and other duty-bearers.
3. Participation	Ensure participation is active, free and meaningful - including communities, civil society, minorities, women, children and others. Mere formal consultation is not sufficient. Ensure that national and local development processes and institutions are accessible and that information is transparent and timely.
4. Non-discrimination & prioritisation of vulnerable groups	Address, as a priority, discrimination and protect vulnerable groups. Who is vulnerable here and now is a question to be answered on national and local levels. Ensure official data is disaggregated, by religion, ethnicity, language, sex, migrant status, age and any other category of human rights concern. Ensure gender-proofing is part of the wider human rights-proofing of all programming (noted in principle 1. above). Gender-proofing assesses the implications for women and men of any planned action, including policies, legislation and programmes, in any area and at any level. Pay particular attention to the "feminization" of poverty, its causes and remedies.
5. Accountability	Apply human rights impact assessment to all plans, proposals, policies, budgets and programmes to determine progress in human rights terms. Identify both positive obligations of duty-holders (to protect, promote and provide) and negative obligations (to abstain from violations) of the full range of relevant actors, including local authorities and private companies. Identify claim-holders (and their entitlements) and corresponding duty-holders (and their obligations). Translate universal standards into Irish benchmarks for measuring progress and enhancing accountability. Develop effective laws, policies, institutions, administrative procedures and mechanisms of redress that ensure delivery of entitlements, respond to denial and violations, and ensure accountability.

Endnotes

2. E.g. UN General Assembly Resolutions (which might be called "UN Principles", "UN Standard Rules", etc.) are "soft law" and, while instructive as to how states can meet their binding obligations, are considered non-binding.

3. A/CONF.157/24 (Part I), Chapter III.

4. www.unhchr.ch/huridocda/huridoca.nsf/(Symbol)/A.CONF.157.23.En?OpenDocument

5. The inverse relationship has also been documented, e.g. with those with mental illness at increased risk of homelessness.

6. While Governments have the primary responsibility for protecting the human rights of their population, international obligations already extend beyond states to private individuals, e.g. for international crimes under the Rome Statute of the International Criminal Court.

7. Economic non-state actors, such as companies and international financial institutions, are also accountable for the human rights impact of their activities under the UN Norms on the Responsibilities of Transnational Corporations and Other Business Entities with Regard to Human Rights, E/CN.4/Sub.2/2003/12/Rev.2.

8. General Comment 14, *The Right to the Highest Attainable Standard of Health* (Article 12).

9. *Guerra and Others v Italy*, 1 ECHR 14967/89, judgement of 19 February 1998.

10. UN Human Rights Committee in *Apirana Mahuika et al v New Zealand* (CCPE/C/70/D/547/1993).

11. For example, European Court of Human Rights, *Lopez-Ostra v Spain*, (Series A, Vol 303, Judgment of 8 June 1995 ; Guerra and Others v Italy (Reports 1998-I, Judgment of 19 February 1998).

12. Norms on the Responsibilities of Transnational Corporations and Other Business Entities with Regard to Human Rights, E/CN.4/Sub.2/2003/12/Rev.2 .

13. Adopted by more than 178 Governments at the UN Conference on Environment and Development (UNCED) held in Rio de Janerio, Brazil, 3 to 14 June 1992.

14. Conclusions, Meeting of Experts on Human Rights and the Environment, 14-15 January 2002, in accordance with Decision 2001/111 of the UN Commission on Human Rights.

15 GA Resolution 41/128 of 4 December 1986. www.unhchr.ch/html/menu3/b/74.htm

16. UN World Commission on Environment and Development, Brundtland Report (1987) *Our Common Future* (A/42/427).

17. Commission on Human Rights Resolution 2003/71.

18 It is sometimes referred to as human rights "mainstreaming" or "integrating" human rights. In this document the expression "human rights based approaches" is used in the plural to reflect the fact that different approaches can be applied.

19. The UK Department for International Development, for example, uses as its over-arching principles, *Participation, Inclusion and Fulfilling Obligations* to encapsulate its commitment to HRBA. On the other hand, the UN HURIST Programme uses the acronym PANEL representing *Participation; Accountability, Non-discrimination, Empowerment, Linkage to normative standards*. For a range of definitions employed by various actors see http://www.crin.org/docs/resources/publications/hrbap/Interaction_analysis_RBA_definitions.pdf.

20. ODI Briefing Paper 3, *What can we do with a Rights-Based Approach to Development?*, September 1999.

21. Opening statement to the General Assembly Special Session on Social Development, Geneva, June 2000.

22. Table 1 is distilled and adapted from the work of OHCHR on HRBA, see Annex 1.

Today there is consensus among states regarding the universal framework and core standards that international human rights entail. It is perhaps best illustrated by the near universal[23] adoption by the world's states, including Ireland, of the UN Convention on the Rights of the Child as binding minimum standards governing States. From agreement on the core standards in the various treaties, attention has increasingly turned to the effective implementation of such standards, and the tools and mechanisms necessary to achieve this.

While a range of actors have made important contributions to the evolution of HRBA concepts and practices, the role of the United Nations (UN) has been central. Development agencies of the UN system, especially the UN Development Programme (UNDP),[24] have long pioneered people-centred approaches. This is not surprising, as the UN organization and its member states are charged with collective and individual responsibility to promote universal respect for human rights. This is a founding principle and purpose of the UN.[25] The full integration of human rights throughout the UN system is, and always has been, a legal imperative flowing from the UN Charter.

The acknowledgment that the enjoyment of human rights is *both the means and the goal* of development is therefore of long standing, and the concept of human rights based approaches is not new.[26] This policy commitment was reaffirmed by the UN system as a whole in its 1997 Programme of Reform for all parts of the system, from the UN Development Programme to the World Bank.[27] This reform programme drew on the UN Declaration on the Right to Development of 1986, which indicated the necessity of a human rights framework for effective development. A similar commitment to HRBA is reflected in the 1990s world conferences on social development, gender, human rights and racism, as well as in the Millennium Development Goals agreed by UN members in 2000.[28] In 2003, UN agencies agreed a Common Understanding of HRBA in the context of their development cooperation and programming, including key elements of best practice as regards HRBA.

Leading development NGOs, such as Oxfam, ActionAid International, and Care International also work to apply HRBA – acknowledging the imperative of being human rights implementing

agencies as opposed to providers of charity. Not only NGOs active in development but also many engaged in humanitarian response and peace processes see the added value of human rights based approaches in securing sustainable solutions. The largest combined aid donor in the world, the EU, has committed to apply human rights in its aid relationships with non-EU countries, through implementation by the European Commission and its country-level offices world-wide.[30] A range of bi-lateral donor states (such as the UK, Sweden, the Netherlands and Denmark), as well as regional organizations take a similar approach. A wide range of international

Bono from Irish rock group, U2, with former President of Ireland and United Nations High Commissioner for Human Rights, Mary Robinson, at the launch of The Human Development Report 2003 by the UN Development Programme, in Government Buildings, Dublin on 8th July 2003.

© *Eamonn Farrell/Photocall Ireland*

actors have now made explicit their legal and policy commitment to base their development work on human rights standards. Changing practices to reflect these commitments is, however, a slow process of learning from experience.

3.1 Progress in international practice

An established body of HRBA experience is available from a range of states and other actors. Some of these are outlined in the resource materials in Annex 1. Some illustrations of this experience are outlined here, while this chapter concludes by asking what difference do human rights based approaches make.

Efforts to apply HRBA have seen a range of actors revisiting policies, practices and institutional structures in moving beyond recognition in principle that their work should be based in human rights. It has included development of methodologies and practical tools. Some of these initiatives are led by multi-lateral agencies; others are the result of national efforts. In some cases, the way is being led by NGOs, academics or community groups – in others, states take the lead though ministries responsible for national planning or various sectors (health, education, environment, etc.).

A number of bilateral donors have also been to the forefront in making human rights based approaches central to their overseas development programming, including the international development agencies of Canada (CIDA), Norway (NORAD), Denmark (DANIDA), and Sweden (SIDA), and the UK Department for International Development (DfID).

Within the UN system, the United Nations Children's Fund (UNICEF)[31] has led the way in developing programming tools and placing human rights at the centre of assessing its own impact. The World Health Organization (WHO) supports governments towards applying HRBA

To say that CARE is a human rights organization ... does not mean that we have embraced a human rights approach. How is a "human rights approach" to our work different? A human rights approach for CARE would mean that we view people we assist as rights-holders and not simply beneficiaries or participants. Our central aim – across all our programmes – would be to facilitate, in collaboration with others, a process of self-empowerment of poor, disenfranchised peoples and communities in order to help them pursue and achieve progressively their rights, broadly defined, as human beings.

Care International
www.kcenter.com/phls/r
ba.htm

UN General Assembly observes a minute of silence in commemoration of the 60th Anniversary of the Liberation of the Nazi Concentration Camps on 24th January 2005.
© *UN Photo/Eskinder Debebel*

in national health policies and strategies through a designated health and human rights team.[32] A joint UNDP-OHCHR programme works to support national governments in their development planning by developing methodologies and identifying best practices in HRBA.[33]

Of central importance to the evolution of HRBA has been a focus on evaluation and assessment of polices, projects and other interventions in terms of their intended or unintended human rights consequences. At the heart of this is an array of parallel initiatives to develop human rights based indicators and other tools. This involves government ministries, directorates of the European Commission, UN agencies and NGOs revisiting how they determine success or failure and measure the impact of their work.[34]

While the range of work on HRBA has increased very rapidly in recent years, much of it remains fragmented. Pooling of experience and identification of positive lessons for replication remains the exception rather than the rule. In particular, little has been done to transplant lessons from the more extensive application of HRBA in developing world contexts to industrialised states.

Two seminal processes intended to bring a *systematic approach to country level efforts to apply HRBA* are illustrative for the later discussion of Ireland's experience. The first is the UN Development Assistance Framework which is applied in most countries which have UN offices present engaged in development work. The second process is that of National Human Rights Action Plans, which is of more specific relevance to Ireland as it has been promoted by the UN in all countries, regardless of their stage of development. These two processes are potential key tools for applying HRBA at country level. The two processes are introduced here, not to suggest their success in any particular country, but to indicate models for practical approaches to give real meaning to HRBA in Ireland, assuming lessons are learned from their application elsewhere.

"Non-Violence", a large replica in bronze of a 45-calibre revolver, the barrel of which is tied into a knot. It was created in 1980 as a peace symbol by artist Karl Fredrik Reuterswärd, and is located in the Visitors' Plaza of the UN Headquarters in New York.
© *UN/DPI Photo*

UN Development Assistance Framework (UNDAF). The UN Secretary General's reform programme has involved encouragement of the wide range of UN agencies to work together *as a team* at country level.[35] The UN Country Team is expected to agree, in conjunction with the government concerned, a common analysis of the country's challenges and solutions. This analysis leads to a multi-year development plan to frame the government's future planning. Most significantly, this process, intended to shape the vision and allocation of development resources by UN agencies for a period of years, is expressly founded on the human rights obligations of the country concerned, and is designed so as to help it fulfill its obligations. The UN guidelines require that the process be participatory, with civil society input and access to information – not simply a UN-government dialogue.

National Human Rights Action Plan (NHRAP). This is another country-level planning process intended to bring together all relevant national actors to produce a time-bound set of priorities for achieving human rights change. This concept originates with the Vienna Declaration and Programme of Action which called upon states to consider such a process. While the title varies from country to country, such plans have been developed in countries as diverse as Brazil,[36] South Africa,[37] Moldova,[38] Lithuania,[39] Sweden[40] and Australia.[41] An NHRAP is meant to constitute an action-oriented process which includes strong participation, benchmarks and targets along with mechanisms for ongoing monitoring and evaluation. The process itself facilitates national debate on the nature of human rights and the choices to be made. The process is recognised as being as important as the outcome, with participation generally facilitated through committees, public meetings and hearings. Central to NHRAP's success or failure has been the extent to which it is linked to any over-arching development process such as a country's National Development Plan. Equally it needs to be linked to policy planning and budget decisions in sectors such as health, education and law enforcement to ensure that human rights concerns are not "quarantined" as a distinct sector.[42]

3.2 Challenges

A selection of the challenges that typically arise in seeking to implement HRBA or that are raised in opposition to such approaches are mentioned briefly here. Part Two will reflect on the extent to which some of these are relevant to the Irish experience. These challenges include:

Competing rather than coordinated processes

■ The effectiveness of HRBA processes can be undercut where parallel processes are promoted by different bodies. For example, while the World Bank takes part in UNDAF as part of the UN Country Team, it also promotes Poverty Reduction Strategy Papers (PRSPs)[43] with the International Monetary Fund (IMF). The latter does not adopt a Human Rights Based Approach, resulting in incoherent and inconsistent policy processes among donors. This in turn facilitates those governments who wish to play donors off against each other.

Participation not seen as a human right and inadequately applied

■ Where participation takes place it is often ad hoc, seen as involving little more than "ticking the box" and generally favours established civil society actors. As recently as 2004, the World Bank and IMF's Independent Evaluation Office review of their approach to PRSPs noted that "in general the involvement of IMF staff has fallen far short of the active participation in the consultative process and resulting policy dialogue suggested by the policy papers establishing the PRS/PRGF[44] approach".[45]

Weak capacity to undertake HRBA programming

■ This tends to be true both on a domestic and on an international level. It has been known for a UN Country Team to engage consultants to help them draft the country assessment, who were not competent in the human rights framework on which it was to be based.

Lack of clarity regarding the core meaning of HRBA

■ Linked to the challenges outlined above, leadership is needed to help clarify the meaning and implications of HRBA in operational terms. Because OHCHR had few resources to do so, other UN agencies, bi-lateral donors, etc., each reached varying conclusions as to what HRBA means. This has contributed to some confusion as to the essence of HRBA, and undermined the benefits of having all actors moving towards a common understanding of HRBA.

Distorted public perception of human rights

■ In many countries, especially those recovering from conflict or in transition from a particular ideology, the popular perception of human rights has become distorted as

"Poverty eradication is a major human rights challenge of the 21st Century. A decent standard of living, adequate nutrition, health care, education decent work and protection against calamities, are not just development goals- they are also human rights"

UN Human Development Report 2000, a landmark statement on the human rights based approach to development

being related to a particular political ideology or limited to civil and political rights. In other countries, human rights are perceived as a means of protecting criminals from justice.

Low public awareness of human rights and low expectations of change

▓ A root cause of poverty is powerlessness; central to powerlessness is lack of access to information and education. If people are unaware of their human rights they cannot claim them or effectively organise to defend them. Consistent, widespread violations of the human rights of the disadvantaged are abetted by the complacency and apathy of the public at large.

The view that "we cannot afford human rights"

▓ It costs money to realise human rights, particularly socio-economic rights like the right to housing. With the competing demands on limited resources in the national budget, politicians are reluctant to grant such rights, especially when it is hard to assess the future resource implications of such rights.

The view that poverty is by definition addressed by economic growth

▓ Human rights based approaches to development have the potential to contribute to economic growth and the converse is also true. However, it is not necessarily the case that economic growth results in human rights change. Many countries which have seen economic growth have also seen poverty gaps widen where growth in GDP is not accompanied by redistributive policies.

"Let Us Beat Our Swords into Ploughshares"
This bronze sculpture was created by Soviet artist Evgeny Vuchetich and presented to the United Nations in December 1959 by the Government of the USSR. The sculpture depicts the figure of a man holding a hammer aloft in one hand, and a sword in the other, which he is making into a ploughshare. It symbolises man's desire to put an end to war and to convert the means of destruction into creative tools for the benefit of mankind.
© UN/DPI

Endnotes

23. The Convention has been ratified by 192 countries. Only two countries have not ratified: the United States and Somalia. The latter has signalled its intention to do so but the absence of any operating institutions such as a Parliament to ratify the treaty continue to preclude ratification.
24. www.undp.org
25. Article 1 of the UN Charter defines its three purposes: to maintain international peace and security; to develop friendly relations among nations and to achieve international cop-operation including to promote and to encourage respect for human rights and fundamental freedoms for all. Article 55 commits the UN to promote "universal respect for, and observance of, human rights and fundamental freedoms for all without distinction as to race, sex, language, or religion". In Article 56, all UN member states pledge themselves jointly and separately to implement Article 55.
26. For example, the International Labour Organisation, which predates the United Nations itself, has operated within a human rights framework since it was founded in 1919. The assistance programme administered by the UN Office of the High Commissioner for Human Rights (OHCHR) has been based on international human rights standards since 1955. UNICEF explicitly adopted the Convention on the Rights of the Child as its framework for programming as soon as the treaty came into force in the early 1990s.
27. Designed to streamline the UN's work while improving its coordination and management structures, it acknowledged human rights as both a principal goal of the organization and a means by which its other goals could be advanced. *Renewing the United Nations: A Programme for Reform*, UN Doc. A/51/950, July 1997, paras. 78-79, emphasis added, hereafter the Programme for Reform.
28. By 2015, the Millennium Development Goals aim to: 1. Halve extreme poverty and hunger; 2. Achieve

universal primary education; 3. Promote gender equality and empower women; 4. Reduce child mortality; 5. Improve maternal health; 6. Combat HIV/AIDS, malaria, and other diseases; 7. Ensure environmental sustainability; 8. Develop a global partnership for development. For a table of the human rights standards underpinning each MDG, see OHCHR www.unhchr.ch/development/mdg.html

29. *The Human Rights Based Approach to Development Cooperation: Towards a Common Understanding Among UN Agencies*, www.undp.org/governance/docshurist/030616CommonUnderstanding.doc

30. See for example, Communication from the Commission to the Council and the Parliament: the European Union's role in Promoting Human Rights and Democratisation in Third Countries, COM (2001) 252 final, 8 May 2001.

31. UNICEF works for children's rights, their survival, development and protection, guided by the Convention on the the Rights of the Child.

32. www.who.int/hhr/en. A Strategy Unit serves as focal point for developing its health and human rights approach. WHO works to advance health as a human right in close collaboration with OHCHR and the UN's independent Special Rapporteur on the Right to Health. Of particular importance is the human rights based approach to combating AIDs pioneered at the Harvard School of Public Health and Human Rights influencing the UN AIDs agency (empowering women, addressing discrimination, etc).

33. Known as HURIST, the programme's specific aim is to support the implementation of UNDP's undertakings in its policy document *Integrating Human Rights with Sustainable Human Development*. See also, the April 2005 UNDP note of its experience integrating human rights in its own work in *Human Rights in UNDP: A Practice Note*.

34. For example, human rights impact assessment is the subject of an ongoing project coordinated by the Dutch NGO, Humanist Committee on Human Rights, which includes the development of monitoring tools (e.g. Health Rights of Women Assessment Instrument (HeRWAI)) and more generally facilitating information exchange between organisations concerned with human rights impact assessment to identify and measure impact (positive and negative) of policies and programmes.

35. The Country Team members will vary according to the UN agencies present in a particular country, but generally include: the UNDP Resident Coordinator and Resident Representative, as well as representatives of UNICEF, the Department of Economic and Social Affairs, World Bank, International Labour Organisation, World Health Organisation, UN Population Fund, World Food Programme, UN Volunteers, UN High Commissioner for Refugees, the head of any UN peacekeeping/peacebuilding mission, UNESCO and the International Organization for Migration.

36. www.ohchr.org/english/countries/coop/brazil.htm

37. www.unhchr.ch/html/menu2/safrica.htm

38. www.hr.un.md/eng/natz_plan_obz.php

39. www.undp.org/oslocentre/docsjuly03/TomasBaranovas.pdf

40. www.sweden.se/templates/cs/News____10131.aspx

41. www.dfat.gov.au/hr/nap/natact_plan.html

42. See OHCHR *Handbook on National Human Rights Plans of Action*, 29 August 2002, UN Professional Training Series No. 10.

43. Poverty Reduction Strategy Papers (PRSPs) are prepared by governments in low-income countries through a participatory process involving domestic stakeholders as well as external development partners, including the IMF and the World Bank. A PRSP describes the macroeconomic, structural and social policies and programs that a country will pursue over several years to promote broad-based growth and reduce poverty, as well as external financing needs and the associated sources of financing. (www.imf.org/external/np/exr/facts/prsp.htm)

44. Poverty Reduction Strategy/Poverty Reduction and Growth Facility. The latter is the IMF's low-interest lending facility for low-income countries.

45. *Report on the Evaluation of Poverty Reduction Strategy Papers (PRSPs) and The Poverty Reduction and Growth Facility (PRGF)* (2004), www.imf.org/External/NP/ieo/2004/prspprgf/eng/index.htm.

4. What difference can HRBA make?

Proposals for the integration of human rights into development activity can too easily remain at the level of generality – such as being confined to the sweeping commitments in the introduction of plans and policy documents. Development activity does not *automatically* promote respect for human rights simply by expenditure on health, education, etc. Many activities undertaken in the name of "development" are subsequently recognized as ill-conceived where money is wasted, or even counter-productive in human rights terms where certain groups are discriminated against.[46]

As has been emphasised above, there is no single human rights based approach. Rather, as outlined in Table 1, there are principles to be applied to achieve human rights standards. The choice of methods and tools is left to states to choose, according to what is *most effective*. Identifying examples of human rights based approaches which are *effective in achieving positive human rights change* is a question of:

a) Assessing the *human rights impact* of current approaches (taking account of the full spectrum of human rights, the range of affected groups, their specific circumstances, etc.); and

b) Adjusting those approaches through effective learning across all areas of the State's sphere of responsibility.

Former Irish President and UN High Commissioner for Human Rights, Mary Robinson.
© *Eamonn Farrell/Photocall Ireland*

Drawing, no doubt, on her years as a human rights advocate in Ireland, former UN High Commissioner for Human Rights, Mary Robinson, has noted that "a commitment to a human rights-based approach should apply equally to developed and developing countries".[47] Part II of this document, explores the experience of Ireland to date in applying human rights based approaches in its development, reflecting on the five core principles of HRBA: 1. Express application of the international human rights framework; 2. Empowerment; 3. Participation; 4. Non-discrimination and prioritization of vulnerable groups; and 5. Accountability.

In her opening statement to the General Assembly Special Session on Social Development in Geneva in June 2000, Mary Robinson noted that human rights based approaches bring the promise of more effective, more sustainable, and more rational development processes. This added value of HRBA is outlined in the following grid.

Table 2.

Value-added of Human Rights based approaches to development

Greater legitimacy	▮ HRBA are grounded in, and gain legitimacy from, the inherent human rights recognised in international law. These human rights are minimum agreed standards. While human rights are sometimes opposed as western constructs inappropriately "imposed" on other cultures, the legitimacy of HRBA is grounded in their universality which takes as a fundamental starting point the fact that states adhere to these human rights treaties as a matter of choice and as an exercise of state sovereignty. HRBA facilitate greater transparency and wider endorsement of national development processes, as development objectives, indicators and plans are based on the agreed universal standards of the international human rights instruments. HRBA offer an authoritative basis for advocacy by civil society. The relevant international legal obligations empower development advocates to promote basic social services over the sometimes competing interests of those in power. HRBA provide civil society advocates with international mechanisms (both judicial and non-judicial) to highlight policy choices by the State which impede or reverse the progressive realization of economic and social rights.
Greater empowerment & participation	▮ HRBA shift the focus from the fact that the vulnerable in society have needs to the fact that they have human rights. By requiring the meaningful participation of a community (itself a human right), HRBA both require that people be empowered and are themselves a process of empowerment.
Greater coherence across sectors through clarity in establishing standards	▮ The international instruments and the authoritative interpretations of treaty bodies and human rights mechanisms define the content of development (including the requirements of, for example, health, education, housing and governance). These are public, accessible tools detailing the institutional and developmental requirements arising from the minimum standards states have undertaken. HRBA provide a more complete and rational development framework for all areas of human development, whether health, education, housing, personal security, justice administration or political participation. HRBA provide a common template for coherence between all aspects of state responsibility and action (both domestic and external): from the processes and content of macro policy priorities, strategic plans and fiscal allocation, to training and performance assessment of state employees.
Greater relevance	▮ HRBA recognize the multi-level nature of human rights obligations and the need to address them systematically and strategically. HRBA offer a framework for more effective analysis and identify the wider range of solutions needed. Traditional poverty analyses base judgments on income and economic indicators alone. A human rights analysis reveals additional concerns of the disadvantaged themselves, viewing poverty as more than material need but as powerlessness and social exclusion, as highlighted by the World Bank Voices of the Poor study.

Greater impact and sustainability	▓ HRBA offer integrated safeguards against unintentional harm by development projects by ensuring that human rights protection measures are organically incorporated into development plans, policies and projects from the outset.

As an example, economic growth alone is not sufficient to reduce poverty – growth needs to be combined with policies designed to reduce inequality. Donors such as DfID recognise this by a policy commitment to 'broad based economic growth'. Clearly higher rates of growth can contribute to more rapid poverty reduction. Where the income growth rate rises faster, the incomes of poor people tend to also rise faster. However, there is variation among countries in the relationship between growth and poverty reduction. These variations reflect differences in what has happened as regards income inequality – which is central to HRBA concerns to address poverty effectively.

Local ownership of, and participation in, development process, inherent in HRBA, are fundamental to designing development initiatives that are tailored to local realities and needs and maximise impact and sustainability. |
| **Greater accountability** | ▓ By identifying specific duties and duty-bearers, development moves from the realm of "charity" to one of obligation. This includes identifying those responsible for respecting, protecting and fulfilling human rights, and holding them accountable for these responsibilities. HRBA empower communities and individuals to identify relevant duty-holders and assert their rights accordingly.

HRBA require root causes be addressed, which requires the equitable distribution of power and resources based on the recognition that human beings' inherent dignity entitles them to a core set of rights that cannot be taken away. HRBA challenge vested interests and power structures, recalling that development is an inherently political process.

HRBA provide a basis for assessment of development progress made, beyond mere expenditure or increased GDP, and provide a specific set of criteria to which the State and its agents must answer. |

Endnotes

46. See for example the Committee on Economic, Social and Cultural Rights in its General Comment 2 on International Technical Assistance Measures, www.unhchr.ch/tbs/doc.nsf

47. 31(7) *Yale Bulletin*, 2002.

48. States are always encouraged to attain higher standards of respect for human rights, and the law itself is not static - continually evolving as the international community clarifies the content of existing standards or codifies new human rights e.g. with respect to the right to a healthy environment.

49. www1.worldbank.org/prem/poverty/voices

50. For an overview, see *Pro-Poor Growth Briefing Note 1: What Is Pro-Poor Growth and Why Do We Need To Know?*, DfID PD Growth Team, Advanced Draft 12 December 2003; other sources: Lipton and Eastwood, *Pro-Poor Growth and Pro-Growth Poverty Reduction*, presented at the Asia and Pacific Poverty Forum (2001); or Klasen, *In Search of the Holy Grail: How to Achieve Pro-Poor Growth* (2001), paper commissioned by Deutsche Gesellchaft fur Technische Zusammernarbeit (GTZ) for the "Growth and Equity" Task Team of the Strategic Partnership with Africa. See also Dollar and Kraay, Growth is Good for the Poor, World Bank, Development Research Group, Policy Research Working Paper No. 2587, April 2001.

PART TWO:

HUMAN RIGHTS BASED APPROACHES AND DEVELOPMENT IN IRELAND

Part Two examines a range of development issues in Ireland, encompassing economic, social, cultural and political processes from the perspective of the core principles of HRBA. It highlights examples of progress made as well as areas where civil society needs to continue to advocate future action. It concludes with key recommendations for future action to promote human rights based approaches in Ireland.

5. Introduction

Chapter 5 of Part Two outlines the historical evolution of Ireland's civil society actors concerned with human rights and the parallel evolution of the State's commitment to human rights.[51] Following the sequence of core HRBA principles introduced in Part One, chapters 6 to 10 will then identify opportunities and shortcomings in the Irish context, including examples of the value added by human rights based approaches. Chapter 11 identifies overall conclusions and recommendations.

5.1 Evolution of Ireland's commitment to human rights

Rights have been at the heart of those political documents most central to the creation of the Irish State. The 1916 Proclamation of the Irish Republic declared that:

"The Republic guarantees religious and civil liberty, equal rights and equal opportunities to all its citizens, and declares its resolve to pursue the happiness and prosperity of the whole nation and of all its parts, cherishing all of the children of the nation equally ...."

In a similar vein, in 1919 the Democratic Programme of the First Dáil not only laid claim to the political rights of the Irish people but also acknowledged its primary obligation:

The Secretary General of the United Nations, Kofi Annan, at a wreath laying ceremony at the Royal Hospital Kilmainham, Dublin, to commemorate Irish Peacekeepers who have given their lives in the cause of peace.

© *Alan Betson*

"It shall be the first duty of the Government of the Republic to make provision for the physical, mental and spiritual well-being of the children, to secure that no child shall suffer hunger or cold from lack of food, clothing, or shelter, but that all shall be provided with the means and facilities requisite for their proper education and training ...."

The 1922 Constitution enshrined a range of rights and recognised that power derived explicitly from the People – a distinct a break from British constitutional tradition. Its successor, the 1937 Constitution, Bunreacht na hÉireann, also contains a range of fundamental rights in Articles 40-44, including rights to equality before the law, freedom of expression, freedom of religion and the right to education. The Constitution empowers the courts to declare legislation unconstitutional if it breaches these fundamental rights. A range of other rights have been enumerated by the courts over recent decades as being implicit in the Constitution, such as the right to bodily integrity, to marry, to privacy and to free movement.

After independence, this commitment was expressed on the international stage by Ireland's active engagement with core human rights mechanisms. As early as 1923, the new State joined the International Labour Organization (ILO)[52] and, since then, Ireland has ratified seventy-three of its treaties – including its eight core human rights conventions on issues including forced labour, freedom of association, protection of the right to organise, collective bargaining, equal remuneration, discrimination in employment, minimum age and the worst forms of child labour.

While cold war politics saw UN membership delayed until 1955, since joining, Ireland has been an enthusiastic member, rightly proud of the role it has played in civilian and military contexts, such as the peace-keeping contributions of the Irish Defence Forces. Ireland has served on numerous occasions on key UN bodies such as the Commission on Human Rights[53] and the Economic and Social Council,[54] while former President, Mary Robinson, served as UN High Commissioner for Human Rights between 1997 and 2001. A referendum in 2002 saw an overwhelming majority of the Irish electorate endorse the State's becoming a party to the treaty establishing the International Criminal Court to address gross violations of human rights,[55] and an Irish woman, Justice Maureen Harding-Clarke, was among the first judges appointed to sit on the new court.

The 7 Main UN Human Rights Treaties
- Covenant on Economic Social and Cultural Rights (ICESCR)
- Covenant on Civil and Political Rights (ICCPR)
- Convention on the Elimination of all Forms of Racial Discrimination (CERD)
- Convention on the Elimination of All Forms of Discrimination Against Women (CEDAW)
- Convention on the Rights of the Child (CRC)
- Convention Against Torture (CAT)
- Convention on the Protection of the Rights of All Migrant Workers and Members of Their Families (CMW)

For a list of all international human rights treaties to which Ireland is a party, see the Irish Human Rights Commission's website at www.ihrc.ie

Ireland is a party to six of what are sometimes called the "big seven" UN human rights treaties. The exception is the Convention on the Protection of the Rights of All Migrant Workers and Members of Their Families, which is of particular relevance to a growing minority in Ireland. On his appointment as advisor to the UN Secretary General on UN reform, the current Minister for Foreign Affairs, Dermot Ahern, described Ireland as "a small nation with a good history of adherence to UN process". This is at least partly true. But, an example of Ireland's not fully adhering to the UN process is that eight of the twenty-five treaties (i.e. treaties supplementary to the "big seven") identified by the UN Secretary General at the Millennium Summit in 2000 as representative of the UN's key objectives, have yet to be ratified by Ireland.

The Supreme Court sitting in Dublin in 1997
© *Joe St. Leger*

At the European level, Ireland was a founder member of the Council of Europe[56] and has ratified all its core treaties, including the European Convention for the Protection of Human Rights and Fundamental Freedoms (ECHR), and the Revised European Social Charter and Additional Protocol providing for Collective Complaints. It is also a party to the European Convention for the Prevention of Torture and the Framework Convention for the Protection of National Minorities, though it has not yet ratified the Convention on Action against Trafficking in Human Beings adopted by the Council of Europe in May this year. The ECHR has been a guiding authority for Ireland's courts since it was ratified in 1953, even before it was incorporated, by legislation, into Irish law in December 2003.

Ireland's membership of the European Union has also seen expansion of the rights guaranteed, notably in the context of employment and gender equality.[57] The Treaty of Amsterdam, which came into force on 1 May 1999, reaffirms that the European Union "is founded on the principles of liberty, democracy, respect for human rights and fundamental freedoms, and the rule of law, principles which are common to the Member States". Although the EU focus is largely on *fundamental* rights as opposed to *human* rights insofar as they are mainly limited to EU citizens and are largely derived from the requirements of the economic model – as opposed to being recognised as *inherent* to the person – its human rights policy is evolving and gathering greater political momentum. Positive developments include the adoption of a Charter of Fundamental Rights, and the publication of guidelines on a number of human rights issues such as the death penalty, torture and child soldiers. The EU Network of Independent Experts in Fundamental Rights publishes annual reports on the human rights situation in member states. Other commitments arise from Ireland's membership of the fifty-five member state Organization for Security and Co-operation in Europe.[58]

Positive aspects of Ireland's embracing the international human rights framework need to be set against a range of domestic failings. For a period of fifty-six years after 1939, the State functioned under a declaration of emergency with all the limitations on rights that entailed, culminating in high profile miscarriages of justice.[59] Ireland has a legacy of grave human rights failings: for instance, children in the care of the state were sexually abused and used as forced labour, and the State, through its law enforcement agencies, failed to protect children more generally from abuse. Throughout the history of the State, the treatment of women, Travellers,

people held in psychiatric institutions, religious minorities and others have contravened Ireland's human rights obligations. The failure of the state to provide for diversity in its health and education services,[60] and the political corruption and clientelism which has undermined democratic institutions have also contributed to this situation.

Recent years have seen progress and redress in some of these areas and the peace process in Northern Ireland has meant the lifting of emergency legislation.[61] Recent economic progress has also been accompanied by the adoption of a range of new legislation, mechanisms, and institutions aimed at vindicating human rights. This progress, routinely praised by international human rights bodies, includes new legislation (e.g. combating domestic violence, introducing a minimum wage, and prohibiting corporal punishment in schools) and the establishment of institutions such as the Equality Authority, the Irish Human Rights Commission and redress tribunals.

Senator David Norris, who successfully challenged Irish law criminalising homosexuality in the European Court of Human Rights in Strasbourg.

© *Gareth Chaney/Photocall Ireland*

However, it is notable that external factors have been vital in stimulating human rights change in Ireland. Much social progress is linked to requirements arising from European Community law such as the revised National Anti-poverty Strategy; incorporation of the ECHR and the recent establishment of the Irish Human Rights Commission derive from the Good Friday Agreement; a range of civil and political rights have been the result of individuals being forced to engage in protracted litigation before the European Court of Human Rights in Strasbourg.[62] But, while the Human Rights Commission has published extensive conclusions outlining non-compliance with human rights standards in legislative proposals,[63] and the Equality Authority has made recommendations as to how equality legislation should be strengthened,[64] many of their recommendations have not been reflected in new laws. The adequacy of their funding has also been questioned, and the Government has been instructed by the UN to adequately resource these, and other newly established institutions in the field of human rights and non-discrimination, "in order to enable them to efficiently and effectively exercise their duties and functions".[65]

As mentioned earlier, by ratifying UN and Council of Europe conventions, Ireland undertook to comply with their provisions by respecting, protecting and fulfilling the rights they contain. However, Ireland's compliance with these standards remains poor. A range of recent reviews and reports, such as the 2004 US State Department's *Country Reports on Human Rights Practices*,[66] the EU Network of Independent Experts in Fundamental Rights' *Report on the Situation of Fundamental Rights in Ireland in 2003*,[67] and miscellaneous UN and Council of Europe reports indicate a mixture of progress and regression in recent years.

Several specific recommendations from UN and Council of Europe committees have been ignored. For instance, despite the clear recommendation of the UN Committee on Economic, Social and Cultural Rights,[68] the Disability Act, 2005 is not human rights based, and does not adequately provide for the core minimum or progressive realization of economic and social rights of people with disabilities. The Government has also failed to establish independent and impartial inspection and complaints mechanisms for prisoners, as recommended by the European Committee for the Prevention of Torture in reports of successive visits to Ireland in 1993, 1998, and 2002.[69] Rather than repeal the Offences Against the State Acts and abolish the Special Criminal Court, as recommended by the UN Human Rights Committee in 2000, the Government introduced wider powers under the 1998 Amendment Act, and provided for a second Special Criminal Court in the Criminal Justice Act 2004.

Members of various disability groups marching through Dublin to the Dáil in 2005 where they voiced their opposition to the Disability Bill for failing to adopt a human rights based approach.

© *Lar Boland/Photocall Ireland*

Recent reports from expert bodies highlight current concerns. In 2004, the European Committee of Social Rights issued its conclusions on Ireland's first report under the Revised European Social Charter, finding 12 cases of non-conformity with the Charter, including failures to comply with its obligations in the employment of children and towards migrant workers.[70]

The UN Committee on the Elimination of Racial Discrimination, in its 2005 concluding observations on Ireland's first periodic report, expressed concern about the treatment of asylum seekers, failure to prevent the exploitation of migrant workers, and questioned the effectiveness of policies and measures to improve access by the Traveller community to health services, housing, employment and education.[71]

Also in 2005, the UN Committee on the Elimination of Discrimination against Women was critical of the persistence of traditional stereotypical views of the social roles and responsibilities of women, reflected in Article 41.2 of the Constitution, in women's educational choices and employment patterns, and in women's low participation in political and public life.[72] It expressed its concern at the prevalence of violence against women and girls in Ireland, low prosecution and conviction rates of perpetrators, high withdrawal rates of complaints, inadequate funding for organizations that provide support services to victims, and the failure to address trafficking of women and children into the state.

While pointing to progress in establishing an independent Garda Ombudsman Commission and Ombudsman for Children, Amnesty International's entry on Ireland in its annual report for 2004, observes serious human rights concerns including: persistent allegations of ill-treatment by Gardaí; unsatisfactory conditions for the care and treatment of people in mental health in-patient units, with a severe shortage in mental health services for young people resulting in children being detained in adult psychiatric hospitals; and prison conditions that do not comply with international standards on humane detention, with overcrowding, lack of adequate sanitation facilities, insufficient education and employment programmes, and mentally ill prisoners held in padded cells in prisons rather than in specialized mental health facilities.[73]

Rights and Justice Work in Ireland: a New Base Line Report (2001), succinctly maps the background to the human rights situation in Ireland:[74]

"Ireland in recent years has experienced modest population growth, immigration overtaking emigration, dramatic and sustained levels of economic growth, persistent poverty and widening of inequality. Ireland's health and social indicators reveal a dismal picture, and the level of investment in public services is low. ... Ireland's record on civil rights, human rights and related issues falls far short of international human rights standards."

Children from the Traveller Community let their wish balloons fly, on behalf of the Irish Traveller Movement (ITM), to mark International Human Rights Day, Millennium Bridge, Dublin in 2004

© *Graham Hughes/Photocall Ireland*

This 2001 report also concludes that, while the role of the voluntary and community sector in Irish society has been more fully recognized by government, the sub-sector employing human rights based approaches in their work is unusually small by international comparisons:

"There are relatively few rights and justice voluntary organizations, but between them they cover a wide range of issues. Many have been imaginative and resourceful, achieving much with little. There are groups concerned with social exclusion and the rights of excluded groups, with ethnic minorities, refugees and asylum seekers (a fast growing area), with political accountability and new democratic ideas. Funding for the voluntary sector in Ireland has improved, but rights and justice organizations are relatively poorly resourced."

5.2 Civil Society and human rights in Ireland

There is no single agreed definition of the concept of "civil society". However, it is generally regarded as including a range of organizations and bodies engaged in public activities, other than the State or its agents. As well as the general public, the term includes "non-governmental organizations" (NGOs) as well as the media, trade unions and churches.[75] In turn, human rights NGOs represent a sub-set of NGOs more generally.[76]

Much of the stimulus for human rights reform in Ireland can be traced to civil society actors, sometimes small organizations, or committed individuals. Historical precedents of individuals mobilising the wider society abound - teenager Rosie Hackett, organizing women workers in Jacobs' factory in 1913 or Dunne's Stores worker, Vonnie Munroe, refusing to handle apartheid produce in 1984. The vibrancy of civil society in Ireland might be seen to derive from an embedded culture of humanitarianism and historical political consciousness. Civil society actors, influenced by secular and religious thinking, have been active across the full spectrum of human rights since the foundation of the State; challenging discriminatory laws and policies and excessive emergency powers, campaigning for social welfare provision, for the protection of the environment, for the promotion of the national language etc., as well as for cross-cutting issues such as equality. Some NGOs have an ongoing focus on human rights relating to the conflict in Northern Ireland while others focus on the human rights situations in countries such as El Salvador, South Africa, Tibet and East Timor. Some NGOs are Irish branches of larger international organizations or have partner organizations in Northern Ireland or elsewhere. In terms of legal status, they range from charities and not-for-profit organizations to more informal groupings such as community groups.

A range of organizations working within and outside Ireland, explicitly situate their work within a human rights framework e.g. the Irish Council for Civil Liberties, Pavee Point, Action from Ireland (AFRI), Amnesty International, the Immigrant Council of Ireland and the Irish Commission for Justice and Peace.

An explicit focus on human rights in Irish civil society can be traced along a continuum that includes the women's movement, campaigners for disability rights, the Traveller community and more recently, groups addressing migrants' rights, racism and the environment. The landscape of civil society in Ireland today includes a range of NGOs campaigning for the incorporation into Irish law of human rights treaties which Ireland has ratified, as well as the requirements and recommendations arising from such treaties. These include the Children's Rights Alliance campaign for the implementation of Ireland's obligations under the Convention on Rights of the Child, and the Women's Human Rights Alliance.[77]

> "Within [Traveller organizations] there has been an important shift in emphasis from a welfare approach inspired by charity to a rights-based approach inspired by a partnership process, in working to improve the life circumstances of Travellers."
>
> **Department of Education and Science,** *Guidelines on Traveller Education in Primary Schools,* **2002**

Members of the Traveller Community and their supporters in Dublin, 2002, protest against the Housing (Miscellaneous Provisions) No. 2 Bill which, despite the Government's failure to meet its Traveller accommodation targets, extended local authorities' powers to move Travellers from public land and made trespass to land a criminal offence.

© *Irish Times/David Sleator*

Central to the emergence of these human rights based campaigns is the recognition of the universality of human rights. This is illustrated by the transition from collecting "pennies for black babies" to the wider focus on social justice and the root causes of poverty by the late Fr Niall O'Brien in the Philippines and the justice-based Lenten campaigns of Trócaire. In 1975, Comhlámh, an association of Irish returned development workers was established to promote understanding of the links between domestic issues in Ireland and overseas development – raising awareness of the universality of human rights.

In addition, formal or ad hoc alliances have emerged around ongoing human rights issues like homelessness, juvenile justice, and proposed Anti-Social Behaviour Orders. In 2005, an alliance of some forty groups concerned with anti-racism, community development and human rights, published a Shadow Report in response to Ireland's first report to the UN Committee on the Elimination of Racial Discrimination.[78]

Despite these various alliances and the increased use by NGOs of human rights arguments it remains debatable whether one can accurately refer to an Irish "human rights movement". Irish society at large, including many NGOs themselves, continue to view human rights actors in Ireland in narrow terms, confined to organizations working overseas or those with "human rights" in their title. It remains the case that organizations that describe their goals in human rights terms continue to be a small sub-set of civil society. The *Comhairle Directory of National Voluntary Organizations* for 2004-2005 illustrates the point. Some five hundred NGOs and social service agencies comprising support groups, charities and campaigning groups are listed. Of those listed, a total of fourteen organizations refer to "human rights" or a specific international human rights framework for their work with an equal number making reference to their focus on the "rights" of a specific group.

"Share the Wealth" rally outside the Oireachtas in Dublin, organised by the National Anti-Poverty Networks in 1999.

© *Irish Times/Paddy Whelan*

There is a visible trend of a range of organizations being conscious of the need to go further in developing their human rights thinking. Despite the pressures of resources and expertise, NGOs are increasingly training themselves in and employing human rights based approaches, and engaging in alliances to this end. This entails NGOs reviewing their objectives, working practices, relationships, benchmarks and indicators to integrate human rights in their work. Current initiatives include collaboration between those civil society actors who are traditionally understood as human rights organizations and others coming from a poverty or community perspective. These include the Human Rights Based Approach Initiative, for which Amnesty International commissioned this document, as well as the Participation and the Practice of Rights Project, which seeks to address social and economic exclusion through the norms and practice of human rights.

Endnotes

51. This document focuses on the Republic of Ireland, as opposed to the island as a whole, due to the relatively few, though increasing, island-wide development processes.
52. www.ilo.org
53. www.unhchr.ch/html/menu2/2/chr.htm
54. www.un.org/docs/ecosoc
55. Rome Statute of the International Criminal Court, UN Doc. 2187 UNTS 90, entered into force 1 July 2002.
56. www.coe.int
57. For an account of current concerns in the EU human rights agenda, see *Deliver on human rights: Amnesty's appeal to the UK Presidency of the EU* (AI Index: IOR 61/017/2005), Amnesty international EU Office, June 2005, www.amnesty-eu.org
58. The OSCE Office for Democratic Institutions and Human Rights (ODIHR) monitors, and reports on, compliance by participating States with their human dimension commitments, particularly in the areas of freedom of assembly and association, the right to liberty and to a fair trial, and in the use of the death penalty. See www.osce.org
59. For example, following his conviction for involvement in the 1976 Sallins Train Robbery Nicky Kelly was given a presidential pardon in 1992 and received £750,000 in compensation.
60. For example, the UN Committee on the Elimination of Racial Discrimination recently noted "that almost all primary schools are run by Catholic groups and that non-denominational or multidenominational schools represent less than 1 per cent of the total number of primary education facilities", and "existing laws and

practice would favour Catholic pupils in the admission to Catholic schools in case of shortage of places, particularly in the light of the limited alternatives available". It recommended "the establishment of non-denominational or multidenominational schools and to amend the existing legislative framework so that no discrimination may take place as far as the admission of pupils (of all religions) to schools is concerned". Concluding observations of the Committee on the Elimination of Racial Discrimination: Ireland, 14/04/2005.

61. Emergency Powers Act, 1976, rescinded in 1995.

62. E.g. *Norris v. Ireland* (1989) 13 EH RR 185, *Airey v Ireland* (1979) 2 EHRR 305.

63. See www.ihrc.ie

64. E.g. *Overview of the Employment Equality Act 1998 and the Equal Status Act 2000 in light of the Transposition of the European Union 'Race' Directive (RD), Framework Employment Directive (FED) and the Gender Equal Treatment Directive (GETD)*, Equality Authority (2003).

65. Concluding observations of the Committee on the Elimination of Racial Discrimination on Ireland's initial and second periodic reports, CERD/C/IRL/CO/2.

66. dublin.usembassy.gov/ireland/human_rightsrep.html

67. europa.eu.int/scadplus/leg/en/lvb/r10114.htm

68. Concluding Observations of the Committee on Economic, Social and Cultural Rights: Ireland, 5 June 2002, E/C.12/1/Add.77.

69. CPT/Inf (95) 14, published on 13 December 1995; CPT/Inf (99), published on 17 December 1999; and CPT/Inf (2003) 36, published on 18 September 2003.

70. European Committee of Social Rights Conclusions 2004 (Ireland).

71. Note 16 above.

72. Concluding comments on Ireland's fourth and fifth periodic reports, C/IRL/4-5/CO.

73. Amnesty International Report 2005: The State of the World's Human Rights (AI Index: POL 10/001/2005). web.amnesty.org/report2005/irl-summary-eng

74. Harvey, Joseph Rowntree Charitable Trust (2001).

75. An NGO is commonly understood as an independent association of people acting together for some common purpose, other than achieving public office, making profit or pursuing illegal activities.

76. The concept of human rights NGO is used here to signify a non-governmental organization whose ethos and policy positions derive from the concept of human rights (as opposed to welfare or charity etc), and which works to promote human rights generally, a particular human right as such (e.g. the right to health), or the human rights of a particular group (e.g. workers, children), domestically or internationally.

77. An initiative of the Pro-Beijing Women's NGO Coalition (chaired by NWCI), the WRHA campaigns for the implementation of the UN Beijing Declaration and Platform for Action and other international commitments on women's human rights, including CEDAW. (www.whra-Ireland.org)

78. NGO Alliance Shadow Report: In Response to the Irish Government's First National Report to CERD under the United Nations International Convention on the Elimination of All Forms of Racial Discrimination (November 2004).

79. This project comprises human rights, community, and anti-poverty groups as well as trade unions and state agencies in the Republic and Northern Ireland: the Combat Poverty Agency, Community Foundation, the Committee for the Administration of Justice, Dublin Inner City Partnership, and the Irish Council for Civil Liberties.

6.1 Definitions and core principles

Fundamentally, Human Rights Based Approaches (HRBA) require recognition that a particular objective, even if presented as a political commitment or policy goal, may in fact be a binding legal obligation. Thus, HRBA require awareness and acknowledgment of a range of binding legal obligations. These obligations include not only the treaties, but also the jurisprudence and other commentaries which have elaborated upon treaty provisions over the past 50 years, since the adoption of the Universal Declaration of Human Rights.[80] The framework also includes a range of principles, indicators and other tools for achieving and measuring human rights impacts. To comply with Ireland's treaty obligations, the State's policies and programmes must be explicitly based on this framework.

The express application of the human rights framework goes beyond citing a particular human right or treaty and necessitates recognition of the inter-related and interdependent nature of human rights. The illustration of the right to health below highlights this inter-relationship and interdependence. As part of the UN system, the WHO recognises the human rights basis of its work. The following diagram (adapted from WHO materials) illustrates the legal principle that all human rights are interdependent. In particular, it notes the connection between human rights traditionally classified as civil or political (e.g. right to information, right to privacy, right to participation) and socio-economic rights (e.g. the right to health).

United Nations Secretary General Kofi Annan with An Taoiseach Bertie Ahern TD in the grounds of Farmleigh House, Dublin.
© *Irish Times/Bryan O'Brien*

Health and Human Rights
Examples of the Linkages between health and human rights. *(Graph, right)*

The inter-related human rights factors that affect the right to health are well documented by health professionals and others working on health issues at grass roots level. Those who are disadvantaged economically face barriers to a healthy lifestyle, are more likely to be disadvantaged in terms of education, marginalised from efforts to promote the right to health (e.g. information campaigns), less likely to be able to vindicate their right to health in unsafe workplaces, and ultimately discriminated against in a two-tier health care system.

Various international human rights bodies have emphasised the need for such an integrated analysis of human rights and their inter-relationships. For example, it was an Irish case before the European Court of Human Rights, concerning the failure to provide legal aid for judicial separation, which saw that regional human rights body highlight the error in making rigid distinctions between civil and political and economic, social and cultural rights.[81] The Court declared that "there is no water-tight division separating the [socio-economic] sphere from the field covered by the ECHR".[82] This is of particular significance in light of the fact that this human rights treaty has been incorporated into Irish law, as discussed further in 5.2 below.

In addition to recognising the interdependent nature of all human rights, a commitment to the express application of the human rights framework involves the recognition of each individual's multiple identities. It entails a shift from defining a person by their most evident need to recognising them as the bearer of a range of rights, that are more or less pressing according to their profile and situation – not just a person with a disability, for example, but also a man/woman/child, a worker, a citizen/non-citizen, a prisoner; not just a woman but also a Traveller; not just elderly but also a rural dweller, etc.

6.2 Experience in Ireland

The range of human rights treaty obligations Ireland has undertaken was outlined in chapter 5. Ireland has carried out the necessary steps to be bound by these treaties as a matter of international law, i.e. signing and ratifying these treaties. In each case, Ireland has made a legally binding contract with fellow members of the international community, stating that it meets the human rights standards in each treaty.[83]

However, for key human rights treaties, the most basic of their obligations have not been met – the obligation of incorporation - to make those standards part of Irish law.[84]

Under the Constitution, incorporation of treaties is a matter for the Oireachtas. In some cases the entire contents of an international treaty are transposed into domestic law meaning that the agreement has the force of law within the State. However, this is not the approach generally taken in Ireland with regard to the human rights treaties to which it is a party.

The general failure to incorporate human rights treaties is of particular concern given that existing Irish domestic law does not comply with Ireland's human rights commitments. It is of particular significance in the context of HRBA and development that the most fundamental domestic law of the State, the Constitution, is not in compliance with the obligations regarding socio-economic rights Ireland has undertaken. The Constitution for the most part relegates these to mere "Directive Principles of Social Policy" as distinct from rights that can be vindicated before the courts.

Despite the constitutional position, there are three immediate elements of each binding socio-

> "Ensuring a healthy working environment is not just a crucial health and safety prerogative for management, but it is a very important business issue. A well-treated and respected workforce is a loyal and productive one, which will no doubt go on to achieve greater output, results and profits for the enterprise in which they work."
>
> **Minister of State, Tom Kitt TD, addressing the Dáil in 2003 on the establishment of the National Economic and Social Development Office**

economic human right which Ireland has signed up to respect.[85] Each of these human rights whether health, education or social security, has a **core minimum** which must be guaranteed by the State; resources must be allocated in a manner that ensures **no discrimination**; and the State has an **obligation to take steps** to continually improve enjoyment of these human rights. These obligations have consequences for planning, management of resources, measurable action, accountability, etc. in that Government must demonstrate that it is meeting minimum essential levels of each of the rights for all groups in society, and that it is taking sufficient steps to progressively implement the necessary measures and provide the necessary resources for the full realisation of these rights. So, while some aspects of socio-economic rights are a matter for progressive achievement, achieving the core minimum of rights, in a non-discriminatory manner, while taking steps towards their full realisation, represent **immediate** legal obligations which Ireland, by becoming a party to treaties such as the Covenant on Economic, Social and Cultural Rights and the Convention on the Rights of the Child, assumed.

The view that *"we cannot afford human rights"* is a common misperception fuelled by misinformation. It ignores the choices Ireland makes when it chooses to prioritise certain matters and how the national purse is allocated. The misperception also fails to recognise Ireland's immediate obligation to take active steps to ensure respect for economic, social and cultural rights. Many other less wealthy countries have taken steps to ensure compliance with their treaty obligations. In South Africa, for example, relevant organs of the State report to its national Human Rights Commission on the measures that they have taken towards the realisation of the rights in the Bill of Rights concerning housing, health care, food, water, social security, education, and the environment. In spite of the relative wealth of Ireland, there is no similar process to ensure that steps are taken, and no such reporting to the Irish Human Rights Commission, for example, by relevant Government Departments.

The expert international committees which monitor treaty compliance have repeatedly called Ireland's attention to two issues: first, Ireland's failure to provide national remedies to address violations of economic, social and cultural rights; and secondly, its failure to frame national strategies, plans, programmes, budgets, etc., so as to ensure the prevention of such violations. These two core failures are reflected in the absence of coherent systematic human rights based objectives, benchmarks, assessment, accountability, etc., in all aspects of national planning.

A) Failure to ensure that the human rights obligations the State has undertaken are accompanied by adequate remedies in national law:

In its Concluding Observations on Ireland's State Report under the Covenant on Civil and Political Rights in 2000, the UN Human Rights Committee positively acknowledged the increased use of the Covenant by the Irish courts as an aid to interpretation, but expressed "continuing concern that not all Covenant rights are guaranteed in the domestic law of the State party".

The State's position on this issue is that the Covenant's civil and political rights are for the most part expressly listed in the Constitution as fundamental rights or have otherwise been developed by the Courts as "unenumerated" personal rights. The State therefore argues that it is redundant to make provision for such rights by way of ordinary legislation as these would be inferior, and subject to, the existing Constitutional provisions.

The State advised the international committee that it opposes, for a number of reasons, the alternative option, amending the Constitution to incorporate fully the minimum international standards it has signed up to. It argued that this would involve duplication or confusion; that amending the Constitution is difficult and that there is a risk that Irish courts would diverge in their interpretation from the international human rights bodies. However, the inconsistency of the State's position is illustrated by the fact that, despite these objections, the Oireachtas in 2003 incorporated through legislation a human rights treaty, the European Convention on Human Rights, as part of the requirements of the Good Friday Agreement.

If the State's reason, however inconsistently applied, against incorporating civil and political rights is that they would duplicate rights in the Constitution, what reasons are given for the State's failure to incorporate economic, social and cultural rights in Irish domestic law? Some of these rights are listed in the Irish Constitution under "Directive Principles [as opposed to rights] of Social Policy", as mentioned above. The courts have interpreted this to mean they cannot be asserted in a court of law by individuals.[86] In principle, this second-class treatment of economic, social and cultural rights violates Ireland's treaty obligations. This has led the UN Committee on Economic, Social and Cultural Rights to recommend, for example, that Ireland amend the Constitution to ensure the effective enjoyment of economic, social and cultural rights.[87]

The Government has consistently rejected recommendations that ESC rights set out in UN human rights treaties be incorporated into national law, citing the conclusions in the 1996 *Report of the Constitution Review Group*. However, as various commentators have noted,[89] its position is full of contradictions:

a) The Government states that economic, social and cultural rights are not appropriate for inclusion in the Constitution as justiciable rights - yet some such rights are already given this status (albeit more limited in ambit) in the Constitution (e.g. the right to education and the right to property).

b) The Government asserts that economic, social and cultural rights would distort democracy by failing to respect the separation of powers between the different organs of the State. Yet, the experience of jurisdictions such as South Africa and India suggest that Courts arbitrating on justiciable socio-economic rights does not subvert the democratic will. The argument also ignores the fact that decisions requiring resource allocation are made daily by judges. Moreover, this issue has never been put to the people for a democratic choice. The democratic preference on the issue is perhaps highlighted by the election of Kathy Sinnott to the European Parliament in 2004[90] and a recent survey of attitudes in Ireland finding that 90 per cent favour making socio-economic rights a justiciable part of Irish law.[91]

Various arguments against affording equal status to socio-economic rights and civil/political rights with rebuttals are outlined in Table 3.[92] In any event, Ireland is in the position of having signed up to legally binding international standards, and now openly refuses to comply with those standards – a profound contradiction that affects all aspects of HRBA in Ireland.

> Health must be seen "not as a blessing to be wished for but as a human right to be fought for"
>
> **UN Secretary General, Kofi Annan**

Children playing in Ballymun.
© *Irish Times/Frank Miller*

B) Failure to frame national strategies, plans, programmes, budgets, etc., so as to ensure the prevention of such violations.

Given that international treaties do not automatically become part of Irish law on ratification[93] and the failure by the Oireachtas to take the necessary steps to incorporate them, key international human rights cannot be invoked before, or directly enforced by, Irish national courts.

Notwithstanding this situation, there remains an obligation to ensure that Irish law, policies, programmes, institutions and procedures reflect the obligations arising from the range of human rights treaties. At the heart of these undertakings, which are both an expression of state sovereignty and democratic choice, is an ongoing obligation to ensure that institutions, policies and programmes are human rights "proofed". This needs to cover all stages from planning, to monitoring and evaluation with legally enforceable remedies for failure to meet relevant standards.

A roads programme, tax amnesty or privatisation plan may in itself appear to be neutral in human rights terms – but the process of decision-making together with the direct and indirect consequences of decisions taken nevertheless require human rights proofing. Human rights proofing encompasses concerns for fiscal prudence, spending choices in any sector, e.g. the €2 billion spent annually on roads,[94] and has obvious relevance for other sectors and those concerned with human rights. More generally, human rights proofing requires examination of both budgetary process and outcome, including but not confined to positive/negative impact on gender equality, on other vulnerable groups, and on poverty-reduction. This first HRBA principle requires that the full spectrum of human rights obligations which the State has accepted are reflected in all aspects of development processes.

National and local development in Ireland involves a complex range of programmes, oversight bodies, and review mechanisms. This web makes up Ireland's development framework and includes National Partnership Agreements, the National Development Plan, the National Anti-Poverty Strategy, the National Spatial Strategy, and a range of other national strategies covering issues such as decentralisation, children, drugs, women, health and employment. A range of sub-national development exercises include regional programmes, county development plans, etc.

These programmes, with their various direct and indirect impacts on human rights, are currently accompanied to various degrees by poverty and equality "proofing", but their underlying rationale remains that of economics. Programmes tend to prioritise economic growth over the protection of the vulnerable,[95] or the two are identified as equivalent goals without meaningful analysis of the impact of policies on vulnerable groups. Linked to this, existing legal obligations are supplanted in these plans by vague political commitments. *Sustaining Progress 2003-2005*, for example, refers to equality, not as a right of immediate obligation but as merely "*a key goal* which must underpin activity in all policy areas in order to ensure a fair and inclusive society with equal opportunity".

The 2001 National Health Strategy, *Quality and Fairness – A Health System for You*, sets out the strategic direction of the Health Service for the next decade, noting that it is *guided* by the "*principles* of equity, people-centeredness, quality and accountability". In its 1998 concluding observations on Ireland's State report, the UN Committee on the Rights of the Child noted "with regret that a human rights framework encompassing, inter alia, the principles of non-discrimination and equal access to health facilities and services, was not embodied in the recently published National Health Strategy".[96]

The NDP *Gender Proofing Handbook*,[97] refers to a "moral imperative" to gender proof. Suggesting that EU imperatives rather than international human rights treaty obligations underlie NDP gender-proofing, the section on "fulfilment of legal obligations" states: "[T]here are a number of *requirements*, both EU and domestic, which policymakers and practitioners are obliged to fulfil."[98] Neither the Handbook nor the NDP *Toolkit for Gender Evaluation* makes reference to applicable legal obligations, (e.g. CEDAW, CRC, etc.) to the recommendations of the relevant committees or the related HRBA methodological tools developed across the world.

A painted handprint is added to posters in support of United Nations International Day Against Racism in Grafton Street, Dublin, 2000.
© *Irish Times/Peter Thursfield*

In a similar vein, the 2004 Report of the National Economic and Social Council, *Housing in Ireland: Performance and Policy*, notes that, "addressing the broader housing issues, not least the adequacy of supply, will contribute significantly to attaining the policy goals outlined for these particular groups."

In many countries, especially those recovering from conflict or in transition from totalitarian regimes, the popular perception of human rights has been distorted as being related to a particular political ideology (invariably the left) or confined to civil and political rights, etc. As in Ireland, the end result of distorted public perception of human rights is an under-developed public appreciation of human rights and distorted debate on what human rights mean for domestic development.

Far from expressly applying the human rights framework, Ireland's domestic development programmes are marked by a studious avoidance of any reference to the minimum standards binding upon the State. Thus, for example, *Partnership 2000* identifies social exclusion as "imposing huge social and economic costs on our society", but not in terms of rights to be vindicated. Generally, references to "participation", "empowerment", etc., do not acknowledge these as binding international human rights commitments. All of this suggests a gap between these concepts as currently employed and as they would be applied in HRBA (see chapter 7 regarding participation).

A major challenge to advancing HRBA is the failure to use human rights language where appropriate. This is in part due to lack of literacy in terms of the human rights framework, with specialists from other disciplines creating new terms for concepts that are already outlined in international legal standards. Examples include the use of terms such as good governance, democracy and rule of law as somehow distinct goals, independent of human rights, when in reality they are composite human rights concepts. Similarly, commitments to participation, empowerment, etc., are frequently couched in language which avoids any linkage to these concepts as matters of international law and legal accountability. Any suggestion that participation can be achieved without applying HRBA misses the essential importance of the HRBA concept itself. Participation premised on recognition of "beneficiaries" as bearers of human rights is to be distinguished from other kinds of participation (e.g. participation motivated by need for political or other legitimisation) in that it empowers and maximises the

Hilary Rodham Clinton speaking at the Fourth World Conference on Women in Beijing in 1995.
© UN Photo

likelihood of demand for accountability. For this reason, express application of the human rights framework is of fundamental importance as the basis on which the effectiveness of all other HRBA principles depend.

Even national programmes specifically intended to address social exclusion are inconsistent in their use of rights language - if it is used at all. Central to considering whether development planning is based upon a human rights framework is the 1997 National Anti-Poverty Strategy (NAPS). Arising from commitments made at the UN World Summit for Social Development in Copenhagen in 1995, the Irish Government developed this ten-year strategy, which was launched in April 1997. The Cabinet Committee on Social Inclusion has responsibility for the overall direction of the strategy. A NAPS Unit, based in the Department of Social, Community and Family Affairs, is responsible for coordinating implementation of the Strategy.[99]

NAPS is the central social exclusion/poverty reference point for other development strategies and programmes. It adopts the following definition of poverty: "People are living in poverty if their income and resources (material, cultural and social) are so inadequate as to preclude them from having a standard of living that is regarded as acceptable by Irish society generally. As a result of inadequate income and resources people may be excluded and marginalised from participating in activities that are considered the norm for other people in society." The NAPS entails the identification of focal points, and the development of indicators and key targets concerning poverty, health, housing, the Traveller community, people with disabilities, etc. A central role is identified for the Combat Poverty Agency whose 2005-2007 Strategic Plan identifies as a key guiding principle the "recognition of economic, social and cultural rights".

NAPS is a welcome initiative and *potentially* a key element of a human rights based approach. Its definition of poverty acknowledges many of the core concepts that underlie human rights based approaches. Professor Paul Hunt, Rapporteur of the UN Committee on Economic, Social and Cultural Rights, noted this at a 2002 Irish Social Policy Association Conference.[100] Despite its many positive aspects, it is internationally recognised that NAPS does not adequately meet the minimum standards Ireland has agreed to.[101]

It is clear that NAPS is not premised on economic, social and cultural rights, while the vague language used and incomplete list of specified targets dilute the State's legal obligations, e.g. ethnic origin is not included among the equality-proofing criteria. At the first review of NAPS in 2002, *Building an Inclusive Society*, it was merely noted that the "*principles* set out in the International Covenant on Economic, Social and Cultural Rights and other international human rights instruments adopted by Ireland will *inform* the future development of social inclusion policy" [emphasis added]. Similarly, the second meeting of the NAPS Social Inclusion Forum in January 2005 recommended ensuring "that there are linkages between NAPS and the forthcoming National Women's Strategy", but no reference was made to recommendations of the CEDAW Committee or Ireland's undertakings at the Beijing World Conference on Women ten years ago.

A lack of coherence is evident in official descriptions of the nature of NAPS. The 2000 State report under the Covenant on Economic, Social and Cultural Rights describes NAPS as being intended to "implement the United Nations commitment to substantially reduce overall poverty and inequality".[102] However, at the same time, the report describes NAPS as merely an "administrative document" outlining "principles" and "aims", providing a "broad strategic direction". That NAPS is only a strategy statement as opposed to a legal document, is then cited as the reason for not incorporating a human rights based approach.

The State Report, using circular reasoning suggests:

> "... if everyone is deemed to have a right to primary/secondary education ... the expression of such a right does not of itself ensure that the particular needs of 'at risk' students can effectively be met without the appropriate policies."

However, as stressed by Professor Hunt;

> "the integration of human rights into NAPS should not be regarded as an optional extra. On the contrary, the integration of human rights into NAPS is an obligation arising from Ireland's ratification of the International Covenant on Economic, Social and Cultural Rights, as well as other international human rights treaties."[103]

A range of international treaty committees have also made this point in response to Ireland's periodic reports. In 1999, the Committee on Economic, Social and Cultural Rights expressed concern that Ireland had not adopted a human rights based approach in the National Anti-Poverty Strategy (NAPS) and repeated this concern in 2002 when Ireland had still not complied. It urged Ireland to integrate human rights into NAPS, in accordance with the Committee's statement on poverty:

> "In this regard, the Committee reaffirms the State party's obligation to make the Covenant rights enforceable in domestic legislation and confirms that, whether or not the State party takes this step, it still *has a legal obligation to integrate economic, social and cultural rights into NAPS.*"[104]

By refusing to do so, Ireland remains in breach of its essential obligations under the treaty: first, the duty to ensure that national law, policy, programmes, budgets, strategies, etc., all reflect the immediate obligations of the treaty to provide the core minimum of each right and to do so without discrimination; and, secondly the State's longer term duty to direct its planning towards the progressive realisation of those rights.

The same failure has been pointed out to the State by the UN Committee on the Rights of the Child, which noted in 1998: "there is no comprehensive national policy which fully incorporates the principles and provisions of the Convention, encompassing all the areas covered by the Convention. The Committee is also concerned that the welfare policies and practices prevailing in the State party do not adequately reflect the child rights based approach enshrined in the Convention."[105]

Arguments against express application of human rights framework – and their rebuttal
Such arguments as have been presented against the express application of the human rights framework are in large part arguments against the implementation of Ireland's obligations to vindicate socio-economic rights. Some of these arguments are based on cold war ideology and others highlight concerns regarding the perceived economic cost of implementation. [See below Table 3]

> "If we brought in rights-based legislation tomorrow morning, we would be fooling people. We would be putting a template in front of them which the system as we know

it and irrespective of money, could not provide...." The (then) Minister for Health and Children, Micheál Martin, speaking in Dáil Éireann, 12 February, 2003.

Some recent media coverage and statements by politicians, such as that above, indicate a lack of awareness of, often combined with an antipathy to, human rights. This official antipathy is sometimes directed at NGOs advocating human rights – described by the Minister for Justice, Equality and Law Reform as the "self-ordained 'human rights community'"[106] - and to others exercising their human rights, such as peaceful protesters. Human rights, in particular socio-economic rights, are misleadingly presented or interpreted by Irish politicians as representing a challenge to Ireland's economic growth. In an example cited during the compilation of this report, a civil servant from the relevant Department declined to sit on an NGO project advisory board for a review of legislation – the reason given being the predominance of human rights language in the project description.

The failure to base national development planning and resource allocation on Ireland's international obligations raises some fundamental questions about Ireland's position as a party to the Covenant on Economic Social and Cultural Rights ratified in 1989. It also contrasts sharply with the State's policy on its overseas development assistance,[107] as expressed by a member of the same Government as the (then) Health Minister quoted above:

"Ireland Aid takes a holistic approach to addressing the issue of human rights within its development co-operation programmes. The centrality of economic, social and cultural rights, as well as civil and political rights, to all development efforts is not only acknowledged by Ireland Aid but is actively pursued within its programmes. *As the primary focus of the Ireland Aid programme is poverty reduction, Ireland Aid actively works to promote socio-economic rights....*"[108]

Table 3:

Myths about Economic, Social and Cultural (ESC) rights	Reality
ESC rights are qualitatively different to civil and political rights - ESC rights are moral, not legal, imperatives.	▪ Ireland is a party to major socio-economic rights treaties with immediate obligations which it has failed to implement. At the same time its overseas development aid policy seeks to hold developing countries accountable to these very obligations.
	Ireland has recognised the principle of international law that human rights are interdependent and indivisible. In order to provide for the full enjoyment of civil and political rights, the enjoyment of the ESC rights must also be realised. The rationale for this in practice is illustrated by the diagram above regarding the right to health.
	Concepts are distorted and debate misinformed.
	Democratic debate on the merits of ESC rights is missing. In 1996 the All-Party Oireachtas Committee on the Constitution, for example, stated that it would not be considering social and economic rights - in a report about private property.
	The Government asserts domestically that ESC rights are merely moral as opposed to legal imperatives. Yet, the Constitution recognises the right to primary education as a legal imperative, and at the international level it has recognised their legal nature by becoming a party to the treaties concerned.
	Ultimately civil and political rights are justiciable because this is recognised as a requirement of justice and is accompanied by the necessary political will – There is no principled basis to deny the same status to economic, social and cultural rights.
ESC rights are insufficiently concrete to merit equation with "classical" civil and political rights.	▪ ESC rights have been elaborated upon throughout the 20th Century, and as early as 1919 at the international level with the foundation of the International Labour Organization.
	The various socio-economic rights have been subject to decades of elaboration by treaty bodies, UN Special Rapporteurs and case-law. Poverty, for example, has been defined in a range of different contexts.
Concepts such as adequate resources or [according to the Constitution Review Group] poverty are "not susceptible to objective determination".	A wide range of countries including South Africa, India, Brazil, Italy, Finland and the Philippines have made provision at the domestic level for justiciable ESC rights in one way or another. The case-law emanating from these jurisdictions demonstrates that ESC rights are susceptible to objective determination, and would provide useful guidance for the Irish courts.
Judges are ill-equipped to make the kind of decisions required when making decisions in the field of ESC rights.	In any event, on a daily basis judges determine whether a trial or a contract term is "fair", whether force is "reasonable", whether an action is "negligent", etc. There is no logical reason to suggest that Irish judges would have difficulty applying international law concepts such as "adequate" housing, "accessible" education, etc.

Ireland cannot afford ESC rights	▦ ESC rights are largely a matter of progressive realisation and achievement. Furthermore, the international treaties on ESC rights frame those rights as being subject to available resources. This means that the extent of the State's obligations would be determined based on what it can afford.

Vindication of civil and political rights also requires financial resources, in maintaining the criminal and civil justice system (prisons, courts, police etc), providing state compensation for Garda ill-treatment, conducting elections, etc. No politician would suggest that jury trials or elections be abandoned on the basis of the costs involved.

In the face of cost arguments, the UN Committee on Economic, Social and Cultural Rights has highlighted the favourable economic conditions prevailing in Ireland noting "no insurmountable factors or difficulties preventing the State party from effectively implementing" economic and social rights. Ultimately, Irish politicians have the capacity, but not the political will, to vindicate ESC rights. It cannot be assumed that the Irish public shares their view.

In an informed debate, the economic cost of failing to respect ESC rights would be calculated: including failure to prevent crime or adequately rehabilitate offenders, through to the failure to address adult literacy or invest in preventive public health measures.

In fact, enforceable ESC rights have the potential to contribute to economic growth by enhancing relevance, efficiency and accountability in development planning. (See also Table 2 above regarding the value added of HRBA.)

ESC rights are only for progressive achievement	▦ ESC rights entail a number of immediate legal obligations: - Non-discrimination: even limited resources must be equitably applied. - Core minimum of each right regardless of resources, e.g. in terms of health, shelter, education and food. - To take steps: Ireland must progress in the enjoyment of ESC rights according to its circumstances – but not go backwards. It must integrate human rights in time-bound action plans in its development processes.

Justiciable ESC rights are "undemocratic": the Oireachtas not the courts should allocate resources	▦ The implication is that any right that would involve the allocation of resources when vindicated by a court would be undemocratic. Yet the State was compelled to provide resources for free legal aid by the Courts – is the right to free legal aid undemocratic?

Indeed, in any democracy, court decisions routinely have resource implications – the cost of each juvenile detention at Oberstown Boys Centre was recently estimated to be €250,000;[110] the consequences of the finding by the Supreme Court that the State illegally levied nursing home charges has been estimated to cost between €1 and 2 billion. Judgments concerning taxation, compulsory purchase decisions, etc. also pertain to resource allocation.

General Comment 9 of the CESCR on the domestic application of the Covenant on the nature of States parties' obligations notes that:

> "It is sometimes suggested that matters involving the allocation of resources should be left to the political authorities rather than the courts. While the respective competences of the various branches of government must be respected, it is appropriate to acknowledge that courts are generally already involved in a considerable range of

matters which have important resource implications. The adoption of a rigid classification of economic, social and cultural rights which puts them, by definition, beyond the reach of the courts would thus be arbitrary and incompatible with the principle that the two sets of human rights are indivisible and interdependent."

The experience of jurisdictions such as South Africa and India illustrate that having courts arbitrate on justiciable ESC rights does not subvert the democratic will.

Given a recent poll indicating wide public support for justiciable ESC rights, it can no longer be assumed that the Irish public shares the Government's view. Far from being threatened, democracy would be reinforced by a direct vote of the people in a referendum to incorporate ESC rights in the Constitution.

Justiciable ESC rights are divisive and only serve to enrich the legal profession

■ For the most part, people seek recourse to the courts to secure their rights only where the legislature has failed to provide clear rights, so that the boundaries need to be clarified, or where the executive has failed to deliver on the rights that do exist. In Ireland, for example, the vindication of many civil and political rights only followed after litigation in the face of political unwillingness to address contentious issues or matters of concern to women, minorities, and others.

By, human rights proofing policies and spending priorities, the power to pre-empt litigation rests with those exercising political power. If budgets, development plans, programmes, etc., are properly based on human rights then the focus should be on prevention rather than judicial redress.

These are treaties Ireland has voluntarily signed up to. It does not generally hesitate to implement EU obligations – why not these human rights treaties?

Poverty is best addressed focusing on economic growth

■ Poverty is not the only socio-economic issue in question. Furthermore, economic growth alone does not automatically result in human rights improvements. Many countries, including Ireland, have seen economic growth accompanied by widening poverty gaps. This occurs where economic growth is not accompanied by redistributive policies. Corruption, discrimination, and lack of empowerment - all serve to confine the benefits of economic growth predominantly to established elites, which ultimately undermines economic growth itself.

Ultimately, the only coherent explanation underlying opposition to the vindication of ESC rights is that as a society and a State we choose not to prioritise them and choose to remain in violation of international law obligations. Such a position defines the nature of the State Ireland wishes to have and requires a reconsideration of a range of treaties Ireland is a party to or a reassessment of its self-image as a model member of the international community.

The Budget Process

Among the complex web of national and local development processes outlined in this chapter, special attention is needed regarding the ultimate context in which choices are made about Ireland's vision of its own development – the national budget. In some respects the budget is the ultimate indicator of a state's commitment to meeting its human rights obligations. For example, budget decisions are the ultimate litmus test of the State's commitment to address the need for social housing, child care, hospital beds, special educational needs facilities, playgrounds, safe school transport, etc.

There is a variety of aspects to human rights assessment of budget. At its most basic it is an assessment of spending on what might be identifiable as human rights priorities - as against other chosen priorities. This includes direct consequences, such as social welfare cuts. It also includes examining indirect consequences of even apparently non-discriminatory provisions, e.g. choosing indirect rather than direct taxation. A human rights based analysis of the budget also considers the process by which it was produced – such as the transparency of the process, and the opportunities for and levels of participation in the debate (see also participation below).

A range of organizations, State agencies and civil society actors engage on budget issues, from the preparation of the book of estimates onwards. A number also undertake post-budget assessment in terms of whether it is based on the priorities of their sector or target group. Many civil society organizations that do make submissions remain sceptical of the extent to which their input is considered. Some go so far as to say that submissions are as much about visibility before their members as any real expectation of influencing decision-making. Choices based upon political favouritism or the need to bolster electoral support in marginal constituencies are the antithesis of human rights based budgeting.

Budget analysis in Ireland has not been the subject of the kind of scrutiny that is a feature of reviews of structural adjustment programmes in overseas development contexts. Some progress has been made in terms of initiatives to gender-proof, equality-proof and poverty-proof the Irish national budget.[114] Yet these various processes by state institutions and non-governmental actors have yet to embrace a comprehensive, systematic, human rights based approach to assess choices made, with indicators against which progress or regression can be clearly measured, etc.

Just as human rights analysis of the budget does not begin with the publication of the book of estimates, it does not end with the Minister for Finance's budget speech. The process of expenditure of allocated funds (e.g. on social housing), and accountability for this expenditure means that HRBA require an ongoing process of monitoring.

The added value of human rights based approaches in the context of poverty reduction strategies has been enumerated in Draft UN Guidelines on a Human Rights Approach to Poverty Reduction Strategies. These have a specific resonance in the context of the Irish budgetary process. The Guidelines situate poverty reduction as a matter of legal obligation; broaden the scope of poverty reduction strategies to address discriminatory structures; reinforce the binding nature of economic, social and cultural rights; legitimise the demand for meaningful participation of the disadvantaged in decision-making processes; and seek to safeguard against retrogression and non-fulfilment of minimum core obligations. Generally, the Guidelines represent a HRBA framework as a basis for accountability for fiscal choices.

Conclusion

▓ Ireland is in continuing breach of its international human rights commitments, and fails to meet this first core principle of HRBA, in a number of ways:

a) by failing to incorporate key human rights treaties into Irish law and to provide national remedies for violations of such rights, especially economic, social and cultural rights.

b) by failing to ensure that national law, including the Constitution, complies with the minimum standards the State has undertaken on the international level.

c) by failing to frame national strategies, plans, programmes, budgets, etc., so as to prevent violations, and ensure respect for human rights as required by its treaty obligations. Ireland lacks coherent, systematic human rights based objectives, benchmarks, impact assessment and accountability systems, in national development planning.

d) by failing to build the capacity of public representatives, civil servants, etc., to apply the human rights framework in their work (e.g. through training, specialised advice, linking human rights awareness to benchmarking and accountability, etc.).

The express choice not to uphold these commitments has been communicated by the Government to international monitoring bodies. However, the implications appear to be little known or debated, let alone approved, by the Irish public. The issue of public awareness of their human rights and their capacity to demand their fulfilment is the topic of the next core principle of HRBA. The current situation raises some fundamental questions about Ireland's position as a party to major international human rights treaties. As a matter of Ireland's credibility and integrity on the international stage, it should comply with treaties that contain obligations regarding socio-economic rights, including the Covenant on Economic Social and Cultural Rights and the Convention on the Rights of the Child.

The cornerstone for any human rights based approaches in Ireland's development needs to be the express application of the human rights framework. The absence of this impacts fundamentally on the other four key HRBA principles: empowerment; participation; non-discrimination and prioritisation of vulnerable groups; and accountability.

As noted in the next chapter, empowerment is the necessary foundation to enable individuals or organizations to engage in informing and influencing the political choices made in national budgets.

> "The pot of money for the horses and dogs [€69m allocation to Horse and Greyhound Fund] is more than twice as big as the sum allocated to adult education initiatives at a time when nearly a quarter of the adult population is functionally illiterate".
>
> Fintan O'Toole, "Crumbs of Comfort", *Irish Times*, 20th November 2004

Endnotes

80. For example, General Comments of the international bodies established to supervise compliance with the treaties, see www.bayefsky.com/tree.php/id/13/misc/general

81. For an account of the key features of economic, social and cultural rights, and states' duties under international law to take immediate action to respect, protect and fulfil these rights, see *Human Rights for Human Dignity: A Primer on Economic, Social and Cultural Rights*, Amnesty International (2005), AI Index: POL 34/009/2005.

82. *Airey v Ireland* (1979) 2 EHRR 305.

83. These treaties cover both Ireland's domestic and external policies. This is underlined by UN treaty bodies, which regularly make recommendations to Ireland as regards its domestic policies, laws, budgetary priorities, etc. as well as its foreign policy, including overseas development assistance.

84. While some treaties, such as the UN Convention Against Torture and the ECHR have been made part of Irish law, the process needed for incorporation has not been carried out in respect of most treaties – although international law makes it clear that failure to do so, does not absolve Ireland from international

legal responsibility for violations.

85. Outlined in General Comment 3 of the Committee on Economic Social and Cultural Rights, *The nature of States parties obligations*, www.bayefsky.com/general/cescr_gencomm_3.php

86. In *Murtagh Properties v. Cleary*, Justice Kenny held that Article 40.3.1° included the (unenumerated) right to earn a livelihood. This right is included in the Directive Principles of Social Policy which Article 45 puts outside the remit of the courts. Kenny J. argued that Article 45 could be taken into consideration in determining which rights were included in Article 40.3.1°. Interestingly, while Justice Kenny's path has not been followed in Ireland, the Indian Courts have used a similar method of interpretation to circumvent the constraints of their own constitution, which were based on Ireland's Article 45.

87. 2003 Concluding Observations of the Committee on Economic, Social and Cultural Rights on Ireland's Second Periodic Report on the implementation of the International Covenant on Economic, Social and Cultural Rights.

88. See for example, Second Periodic Report of Ireland on Implementation of the International Covenant on Economic, Social and Cultural Rights, E/1990/6/Add.29 reiterating arguments made in its second State Report under the International Covenant on Civil and Political Rights, CCPR/C/IRL/98/2.

89. See, for example, *Completing the circle: making good the UN human rights monitoring system at national level: the case of Ireland*, Irish Commission for Justice and Peace and the Council for Social Welfare (1999); and *Re-righting the constitution - A Case for New Social and Economic Rights: Housing, Health, Nutrition, Adequate Standard of Living*, Irish Commission for Justice and Peace (1998).

90. In 2001, after legal proceedings lasting 5 years, the Supreme Court rejected Kathy Sinnott's argument that her 23 year old autistic son had an ongoing constitutional right to primary education.

91. *Public Perspectives on Democracy in Ireland*, Democratic Audit Ireland project, Tasc (2005).

92. The 2004 All-Party Oireachtas Committee on the Constitution, Report on Private Property acknowledges that the constitutional recognition of socio-economic rights merit "extensive debate" but deferred discussion of claims for constitutional recognition of a right to shelter.

93. Under the Constitution Ireland takes a dualist approach to international agreements which means they do not on ratification become part of Irish law. Article 29(3) provides that "No international agreement shall be part of the domestic law of the State save as may be determined by the Oireachtas."

94. Dáil Debates, 10 May 2005.

95. For example, Ireland's immigration policies and laws have attended to need for migrant workers to sustain the economy without promoting and safeguarding their human rights, such as the right to family in its family reunion policy.

96. Concluding Observations of the Committee on the Rights of the Child: Ireland, CRC/C/15/Add.85 (04/02/98). As outlined in paragraph 54 of the Committee's General Comment No 14 on the right to health.

97. www.ndpgenderequality.ie/publications/publications_00.html

98. Emphasis added.

99. In addition to the National Anti-Poverty Strategy, Ireland also has completed two National Action Plans to Combat Social Exclusion (NAPs/incl), 2001-2003 and 2003-2005. These action plans resulted from the EU Lisbon Council meeting which emphasised the need for the EU to set targets to eradicate poverty and social exclusion by 2010.

100. *Social And Economic Rights: Challenges And Opportunities For Social Policy.*

101. See, for example, 2002 Concluding Observations of the Committee on Economic, Social and Cultural Rights on Ireland's second periodic report on the implementation of the International Covenant on Economic, Social and Cultural Rights, www.ihrc.ie/treaties/treaties_2.asp

102. Second Periodic Report of Ireland on Implementation of the International Covenant on Economic, Social and Cultural Rights, E/1990/6/Add.29, www.ihrc.ie/treaties/pdfs/CESCR%202nd%20Report.pdf. Emphasis added.

103. Note 100 above.

104. (Emphasis added.) Note 68 above.

105. Note 96 above.

106. Address by Minister McDowell at Law Society/Human Rights Commission Conference on New Human Rights Legislation - "The European Convention on Human Rights Act, 2003: What the Act will Mean" on 18 October 2003.

107. The sense that human rights are seen as matter only relevant in the external responsibilities of the State are suggested by the fact that the only Oireachtas committee on human rights is a sub-committee of the Joint Committee on Foreign Affairs. The Department of Foreign Affairs is the only Department with a

Human Rights Committee (comprising Department officials and NGOs). The website of the Equal Status Division of the Department of Justice, Equality and Law Reform makes it only reference to human rights under "International Business" http://www.justice.ie/.

108. Then Minister for Foreign Affairs, Brian Cowen TD, speaking in Dáil Éireann, 9 May 2001 (emphasis added).

109. Note 68 above.

110. "Keeping a boy at Juvenile centre costs €250,000", *Irish Times* newspaper, 12 March 2005.

111. "Nursing home decision could cost €2 billion", *Sunday Business Post* newspaper, 6 March 2005; "Payback for 70,000 in nursing home fees scandal", *Irish Examiner* newspaper, 11 May 2005.

112. www.bayefsky.com/getfile.php/id/367/misc/general, emphasis added. See also, Irish Human Rights Commission, *Observations on the Proposals Paper of the Disability Legislation Consultation Group (DLCG) From the Perspective of the International Covenant on Economic, Social and Cultural Rights*, www.ihrc.ie/_fileupload/publications/DLCG_Observations.doc.

113. Note 91 above.

114. Taylor, *Looking at the Economy Through Women's Eyes*, Banúlacht, (2004) presents a useful model, both in terms of the participatory process by which it was drafted and its guidance on applying a women's human rights framework in budgetary analysis.

115. www.unhchr.ch/development/povertyfinal.html

7. Empowerment

7.1 Definitions and core principles

A root cause of poverty and marginalisation is powerlessness; central to powerlessness is lack of access to information and education. If people are unaware of their human rights they cannot effectively organise to assert them. Consistent, widespread violations of the human rights of the disadvantaged and marginalised are abetted by low public awareness of human rights, low expectations of change and by complacency of the public at large on key human rights issues.

The principle of empowerment refers to the extent to which people are aware of the scope and nature of their human rights and how to effectively demand them through legal and political action. It entails access to information, awareness of decision-making processes, awareness by both rights-holders and duty-holders and, most fundamentally, confidence to claim rights - as opposed to supplicating for charity. The core principle of empowerment is addressed here, in advance of participation and accountability, as it is the foundation on which both these HRBA principles are built. Anyone may choose not to participate in processes that affect their rights, but if they are not empowered to participate, this is not a genuine choice.

Effective training on HRBA is:
- based on the applicable human rights framework
- participatory in its design and delivery
- relevant to the specific situation, roles and mandate of trainees
- part of ongoing process, as opposed to ad hoc events
- evaluated by its demonstrated impact on future behaviour of trainees and improved human rights outcomes for the rights-holder
- linked directly to personnel management providing an incentive to change behaviour, e.g. promotion, benchmarking, etc.
- linked directly to the assessment of the institution/organization's performance (see accountability below)

A human rights based concept of empowerment encompasses not only education and training of vulnerable groups about rights, but also the training of state officials and institutions. Within the framework of the United Nations Decade for Human Rights Education (1995-2004), the UN General Assembly and the Commission on Human Rights called on states to develop *comprehensive, effective and sustainable national plans of action for human rights education.* UN Guidelines emphasise the importance of co-operation by State and non-state actors in this endeavour as well as the importance of ensuring that monitoring and evaluation mechanisms are included in the national human rights education plan.[116]

7.2 Experience in Ireland

At the heart of empowerment is the right to education, including human rights education for children and adults alike. As a society Ireland places great priority on education, though the perception that Ireland has a highly educated population masks the huge divide in education. However, there is acknowledgement that broad sections of Irish society lack empowerment –

"You feel degraded going in. It's like confession...You feel like a beggar on the street."

Combat Poverty Agency Report, *Against All Odds – Family Life on a Low Income,* **describing the operation of the supplementary welfare allowance scheme**

"Despite the committee's concluding comments from the last session, none of the 150+ participants in our consultation received copies of the Convention, the concluding comments, or the general recommendations, and most were unaware of the existence of the Convention at all. Prior to the work of the WHRA, there was no NGO consultation reviewing CEDAW."

CEDAW, Convention on the Elimination of All Forms of Discrimination Against Women: Ireland 2004 Shadow Report **Women's Human Rights Alliance** lack an informed awareness of the scope and nature of their human rights and how to effectively demand them. Despite adult literacy programmes such as those by the Vocational Education Committee, Trade Unions, etc., the stark fact remains that one in five Irish adults are functionally illiterate (22.6 per cent according to the *UN Human Development Report 2005*). For those amongst Ireland's migrant population with poor English language skills, their inadequate access to English language training, and the poor translation and interpretation facilities available to state services, are significant barriers to their awareness of their rights.

Despite the explicit treaty undertakings to do so, and in spite of repeated recommendations by the various UN committees, there is no coherent system for dissemination of the texts of human rights treaties ratified by Ireland, nor of the concluding observations and recommendations which the various treaty committees make to Ireland. Dissemination is passive, requiring people to seek out the information, and is largely confined to Departmental websites.

A number of NGOs and NGO alliances are active in raising awareness of Ireland's duties under various human rights treaties e.g. Child's Rights Alliance on the Convention on the Rights of the Child and the Women's Human Rights Alliance project on CEDAW. Yet, and this is also an accountability issue, there is no systematic State process of dissemination to inform the Irish public, and no national human rights education action plan as the UN has called for. Meanwhile, web sites are often pointed to as if they fulfil obligations to disseminate official information – yet this necessarily excludes a large proportion of the population. This is closely linked to the finding in the previous chapter, regarding inaccurate and the ill-informed statements of some politicians regarding human rights. Challenging such statements requires empowerment of the Irish public and access to the relevant information.

Positive examples of empowerment, based on human rights, include initiatives such as the children's parliament, Dáil na nÓg, the growth in student school councils/elections and programmes such as 'Young Social Innovators' etc. In 1998 the UN Committee on the Rights of the Child recommended that Ireland "promote human rights education in the country and create a wider awareness and understanding of the principles and provisions of the Convention".[117] In particular it highlighted the need for further efforts to develop "a systematic information campaign on children's rights for children and adults alike and the incorporation of children's rights in the curricula of all educational and pedagogical institutions".

However, in the absence of a national human rights education action plan, there is no systematic process to ensure that key public servants (at national or local level) are aware of the nature and scope of their role as human rights duty-holders.

Furthermore, public awareness of even those rights directly recognised in Irish domestic law is regarded as very low. Concerns are raised by NGOs regarding access to information, feelings of exclusion/powerlessness and apathy. The Ombudsman's 2003 Annual Report noted that:

> "Not all complainants have a clear understanding of their entitlements and many of them approach the office with nothing more than a vaguely expressed hope that we may be able to help them...Not everyone who has cause for complaint is capable of articulating their views or understanding complex schemes, rules and regulations. Many

"Advocacy, which has always existed in human relationships is a process of empowerment and can take many forms. It is a way of enabling those who may have difficulty speaking up for themselves to do so and thus can be key to involvement in decision-making. It generally means representing the view of a person or supporting them to exercise or secure their rights."

Jigsaw of Advocacy: A Comhairle Research Report, 2003

Delegates taking part in Dáil na nÓg 2003 at Croke Park where 190 young people from all over the country representing various Cómháirlí na nÓg discussed the issues of drug and alcohol abuse and educational disadvantage.
© *Bryan O'Brien/Irish Times*

people do feel intimidated by the prospect of having to engage with public bodies in order to get a satisfactory service or full and ready access to benefits and entitlements. Generally speaking, the option of redress through the courts is not a viable one for the marginalized in our society."

The National Adult Learning Agency strategic plan 2002-2006[118] refers merely to "needs", "goals" and "aiding the implementation of central Government policy" but studiously avoids reference to the human rights involved or to the fact that its work should be designed to implement the State's international legal obligations.

Empowerment also requires access to information - information necessary to engage with institutions that impact on all aspects of life - including information necessary to build awareness of rights and undertake advocacy. In April 2005, the Information Commissioner criticised what she called an "unwarranted adversarial" attitude demonstrated by the National Maternity Hospital towards her office.[119] She reported that her office had been forced to warn the hospital that it had the power to raid its premises and force staff to provide the documentation for inspection.

In this context, the Freedom of Information Act, 2003, replacing its 1997 predecessor, should be an important empowerment tool. It is noteworthy that the new legislation was drafted without consulting the Information Commissioner. The Act increases fees applicable to information requests and curtails the categories of information that could previously be sought under its predecessor. Regarding the operation of the legislation, the *Annual Report of the Inspector of Prisons and Places of Detention* (2004 – 2005) stated that the Department of Justice "has gone deeper into the bunker since the Freedom of Information Act" and noted a culture of "if at all possible put nothing in writing".[120]

Awareness of and access to information are key elements of empowerment, but they are further undermined in Irish society by the widespread belief that "it is not what you know but who you know"[121] - or where access is predicated on paid membership of privileged circles such as the Forum for Opportunity.[122]

Overall, empowerment in Ireland needs to be viewed in the context of organizations feeling discouraged from asserting the rights of those they represent by the prevailing atmosphere shaped by political leaders. More fundamentally, State institutions have been perceived as threatening those who speak out to criticise policy or provision of basic services.[123]

Tony Geraghty learning to read and write at the Dublin Adult Learning Centre in Mountjoy Square in Dublin. In the background are examples of projects carried out by students.
© *Eamon Farrell/Photocall Ireland*

Conclusion

In violation of its explicit treaty obligations, Ireland has no systematic process for raising awareness regarding the nature and scope of human rights – either for the public or for public servants and other agents of the State. As a result, rights-holders and duty-bearers do not share a common understanding of human rights goals and the duties to respect, protect and fulfil them. While the public remains disempowered, inaccurate and misleading arguments on issues such as the nature of Ireland's obligations regarding economic, social and cultural rights go unchallenged.

Endnotes

116. For guides to organising training on human rights and human rights based approaches workshops, see for example, www.ihrnetwork.org/policy.htm, www.ohchr.org/english/about/publications/training.htm, and www.careinternational.org.uk/resource_centre/civilsociety/basic_introduction_to_human_rights.pdf .

117. Note 96 above.

118. www.nala.ie/download/pdf/streategy_plan_02_06.pdf

119. Office of the Information Commissioner, Case 030830. The case concerned access to documents relating to the retention of human organs. www.oic.iw

120. www.justice.ie/80256E010039C5AF/vWeb/flJUSQ6DVESW-en/$File/ThirdAnnualRpt.pdf

121. An MRBI Survey for RTE's *Today Tonight* programme in November 1991 revealed 89 per cent agreed with the proposition: "There is a golden circle (of business people and politicians) in Ireland who are using power to make money for themselves." The correlation between social deprivation and low voting patterns in elections has been documented in Ireland. Kelleher et al, 'Indicators of deprivation, voting patterns, and health status at area level in the Republic of Ireland', *Journal of Epidemiology and Community Health* (2002).

122. This reported scheme involves 600 businessmen and women being invited to join 'Forum for Opportunity', which involves them receiving access to Government ministers in return for contributions to Fianna Fáil of €1,500 a year for 2005, 2006 and 2007 in the lead up to the next General Election.

123. "Anti-poverty groups criticise funds withdrawal", *Irish Times* newspaper, 25 January 2005.

"One of the worries I would have is that this action was taken by the HSE to shut the parents up! And as somebody who has to fight, push and shove to get the things my son is entitled to it adds a sinister dimension to dealing with the health boards/hse.

Bulletin Board subscriber on 2005 special education needs case of children taken into care by Health Service Executive after parents complained to media over services. Care order later dismissed by District Court. www.boards.ie/vbulletin/index.php

"The World Conference on Human Rights considers human rights education, training and public information essential for the promotion and achievement of stable and harmonious relations among communities and for fostering mutual understanding, tolerance and peace."

Vienna Declaration and Programme of Action

8. Participation

8.1 Definitions and core principles

> The right to participate in decisions which affect one's life is both an element of human dignity and the key to empowerment – the basis on which change can be achieved. As such, it is both a means to the enjoyment of human rights, and a human rights goal in itself.

The five principles which comprise the core minimum of human rights based approaches to Ireland's development are interdependent. As seen above, empowerment is a pre-condition for meaningful participation, while participation is itself a pre-condition for accountability. Participation in all aspects of national development is itself a human right obliging the State to create an enabling environment for participation of all stakeholders.

The right to participation is referred to in specific ways by: the Universal Declaration of Human Rights (Article 21 - the right to take part in the government, the will of the people as the basis of the authority of government, the right to vote); the International Covenant on Civil and Political Rights (Article 25 - the right to take part in the conduct of public affairs, to vote); the Convention on the Rights of the Child (Article 12 - one of its basic principles is respect for the views of the child; and Article 15 - "safe spaces" in which they can be expressed); the Convention on the Elimination of Discrimination Against Women (participation of girls is a principle of "paramount consideration" while article 14 refers to participation of rural women in the public and political life of their communities, and in particular in the design and implementation of development planning).[124]

Participation is a composite, cross-cutting concept, which, to be active, free and meaningful, requires vindication of a range of other rights - freedom of expression, association, assembly, the right to education, the right to receive and impart information, etc. - and is under-pinned by the principle of non-discrimination.

Strong parliamentary institutions are essential elements of democracy, the rule of law – and thus human rights. The Oireachtas is intended to be a central mechanism for participation (and accountability). It is tasked not only with enacting laws but also with mediating differing

> "As States have primary responsibility for fulfilling the human rights of the people living in their respective jurisdiction, it follows that any poverty reduction strategy must be a country-driven process. [....] The strategy has to be owned by all relevant stakeholders within the country, including the poor. This can only be possible, however, when all stakeholders, including the poor, participate effectively in all stages of the process. Active and informed participation by the poor is not only consistent with, but also demanded by, the rights-based approach because the international human rights normative framework affirms the right to take part in the conduct of public affairs. One may distinguish four stages of participation: preference revelation; policy choice; implementation; and monitoring, assessment and accountability."
>
> **United Nations High Commission for Human Rights,**
> *Draft Guidelines: A Human Rights Approach to Poverty Reduction Strategies (2002)*

interests, establishing political priorities and making macro-level resource allocations that directly affect people's lives. Participation also requires input into a range of mechanisms and fora empowered to make decisions which impact on society or particular groups within it, tailored according to specific groups affected and their profile, e.g. children.

International experience suggests that people participate more effectively if institutions and decision-making processes are located closer to their community. This means that local government must have the authority and resources to function as participatory institutions, responsive and accountable to the concerns and needs of individuals affected by its decisions.

Reflecting the importance of the right to participate, it is increasingly recognised in international development practice that public debate, open decision-making, and the organization of interest groups is essential for combating corruption, ensuring accountable policy-making and effective functioning of institutions.[125]

8.2 Experience in Ireland
A past era of deference to religious and political leaders who "knew best" has been succeeded in Ireland by an acknowledgement, in principle at least, of the importance of participation at national, local and personal levels.

At the heart of participation in Ireland is the ever-increasing number of representative groups and consultation processes across a range of policy areas from the EU Constitution and the Government White Paper on overseas development aid to the 6,000 submissions received by the Oireachtas Committee examining proposed changes to the Constitution regarding the family. Much of this participation has been indirect, channelled through civil society organizations.[126] A key player in ensuring participation, the voluntary sector has emerged as a full "social partner" in the European context. While active and committed, as Harvey has noted, "rights and justice organizations are relatively poorly resourced".[127]

Consultation processes now also take place around the preparation by the State of its periodic human rights treaty reports – this is seen as highlighting the potency of international scrutiny. Children's input into the appointment of the first Ombudsman for Children is an example of participation to be built upon – but the UN Committee on the Rights of the Child expressed its concern more broadly that "views of the child are not generally taken into account, including within the family, at schools and in society".[128]

Thus, to be weighed against positive trends, there are examples where consultation is put in place but not respected if views expressed differ from Government. Examples raised include the 2002 appointment of the Irish Human Rights Commission, which saw a committee of civil society consulted then its nominees ignored, before they were included as appointees after an outcry. Other reported examples are the exclusion from the current Social Partnership process of those who declined to endorse the Agreement.[129] Some point to a sense of "scape-goating" of those sections of civil society excluded from Social Partnership processes for failing to endorse its direction. Experiences of some NGOS participating in the government-established

Children playing during break at Monkstown Educate Together National School
© Eric Luke/Irish Times

> "People with disabilities do not want to be pitied nor do they want their disabilities to be dismissed as of little importance. All that is required is a little respect and basic needs and rights. Surely this is not too much to ask?"
>
> **Post Polio Support Group submission,** *Report of the Commission on the Status of People with Disabilities* **(1996)**

Disability Legislation Consultation Group (DLCG), led them to view the consultation processes as amounting to little more than "going through the motions" - a formal process that ultimately does not impact on decisions taken by authorities. Some felt that their significant investment of resources, time and energy had no impact at all. This current lack of meaningful participation is also supported by high levels of cynicism on the part of the public at large, and disbelief that consultation processes impact on decision-making. Most people continue to see the local TD as the most efficient route to addressing their needs. A 2005 Eurobarometer Survey found that while 64 per cent of Irish people professed interest in current affairs, only 31 per cent felt that their voices are heard on public affairs. This reliance on informal contacts privileges those who are connected to or have "pull" with those in positions of power.

For organizations that explicitly seek to apply HRBA in their work, the challenges of effective participation include the need for resources, training and awareness-raising to advocate human rights approaches, including among those they represent.

To be effective, civil society, including human rights organizations, will at times need to work in partnership with the State. In 1998, the Committee on the Rights of the Child welcomed Ireland's willingness to collaborate with NGOs, but expressed its "concern that the potential of the non-governmental sector in contributing to the development of children's rights' policy is not fully realized". The challenge for such partnership is to engage without compromising independence - the essential quality of being a non-governmental organization.

As civil society actors become service-providers for the State (and there are circumstances when they can be more effective than state mechanisms in this regard), State funding involves a risk that such NGOs forego their legitimate advocacy role. A concern that has been raised in recent times is a fear of losing resources if they engage in criticism of policy or failure to vindicate rights.[131] This issue applies to NGOs working domestically no less than those with an overseas focus. Criticisms in 2004 by the Minister of State responsible for human rights and overseas development of Irish aid agencies engaging in advocacy at home highlights a failure on the part of Government to appreciate the connection between distributing aid on behalf of the Government and advocacy to influence Government policies affecting those same recipient countries.[132]

Homeless, and faceless
© *Alan Betson/Irish Times*

Some NGOs will continue to avoid the human rights model as a matter of ideological choice seeing the "political" nature of human rights as negative or as a matter of pragmatism to safeguard their State funding. Others base their work on values inherent in human rights, e.g. consultation/participation, without explicitly situating this work within the human rights law framework.

A perhaps unintentional, but nonetheless unfortunate interference with the advocacy function of Irish NGOs is found in the Electoral (Amendment) Act, 2001. Amending the Electoral Act, 1997, it provides that an NGO (defined as a "third party") may not accept more than €6,348.69 from any one donor in the same year for any campaign which supports or opposes any policy of the Government or a public authority, or any donation for any amount for such a campaign from non-Irish citizens or entities not registered in Ireland. While it might have been founded on the benign intention to safeguard against undue influence in the democratic process, this Act defines "third party" so widely that any NGO commenting on any aspect of Government policy, even favourably, may be caught by its provisions. The definition of "donation" is such that even government funding may be so curtailed, and even if this is found by the courts not to be the case, Irish NGOs are poorly funded by Government and rely heavily on public donations and funding from international philanthropic bodies. Hence, this Act is an unnecessary and disproportionate restriction on NGO funding, and has the potential to seriously hamper their independent monitoring of and commenting on Government policy.

To reflect the HRBA requirement of participation, it needs to be approached as both a means of achieving human rights and as a human right in itself – informed participation increases empowerment and accountability. Yet, meaningful participation requires resources – both in terms of personnel and financial – for civil society and for State institutions. It can slow down decision-making and it presents particular challenges in reaching those who need it most – the most disempowered.

In Ireland's overseas aid policy and practice, participation is seen as essential to enhancing effectiveness, efficiency, sustainability and impact in development planning with partner countries. Yet, in Ireland itself, key issues require reflection and action: who participates? on what issues? at what stages? with access to what information? to what degree of influence?

Conclusion

▓ Participation in Ireland's domestic development is often ad hoc, and superficial - a "box to be ticked" to validate decisions. It is seen as generally favouring private sector or established civil society, who may have a vested interest in retaining the status quo.

▓ There are few examples where participation is well resourced, especially in terms of time. Furthermore, participation is not widely seen as being about well-informed outcomes.

▓ Mechanisms to ensure accountability if participation proves to be less than meaningful, are inadequate.

Endnotes

124 See Kenny, The Right to Participate in International Human Rights Fieldwork, www.ihrnetwork.org/human-rights-fieldwork.htm.

125. For example, the importance of participation is reflected in a process of on-line discussions regarding the World Bank draft World Development Report with independent convenors, begun in March 2000. See www.worldbank.org

126. In addition to civil society organizations supporting participation by a particular group or on a particular issue, The Wheel serves as an independent resource centre on advocacy for community and voluntary organizations. www.wheel.ie

127. Rights and justice work in Ireland: a new base line report, note 74 above.

128. Note 96 above.

129. Sustaining Progress - Social Partnership Agreement, 2003-2005, available at www.taoiseach.gov.ie.

130. www.europa.eu.int/comm/public_opinion.

131. For instance, in respect of community and voluntary violence against women services, the National Observatory on Violence Against Women, in its First Country Report from the Republic of Ireland (2004), points to the "[d]ifficulty of maintaining a critical stance of statutory agency practice whilst negotiating their funding at the same time". www.nwci.ie/documents/irobsvaw04.pdf

132. "Trócaire's Advocacy programme questioned", www.trocaire.org/newsandinformation/overseasaid/tro-cairesadvocacy.htm

"At present there is a major campaign underway to "profes-sionalise" the voluntary sector ... to undertake services that were previously provided exclusively by the State. While this looks like a form of privatisation and partnership, it is probably more correctly described as a form of "nationalisation" of the voluntary sector because it effectively silences once prophetic voices in defence of the most vulnerable in Irish society."

Submission from TRUST - Review of Government's Homeless Strategy (2005).

"Dissent and criticism is increasingly unacceptable"

Sean Regan, Community Workers Co-operative, 2005

9. Non-discrimination & vulnerable groups

9.1 Definitions and core principles

The fourth core principle of HRBA is a cornerstone of the protection of human rights: the prohibition of discrimination in the enjoyment of human rights and prioritisation of vulnerable groups. This is a cross-cutting issue for all human rights as reflected by its express inclusion in all human rights treaties.

Sustained global efforts on these issues have recorded successes. Changes regarding the status of women globally were recorded in the UN 10 year review of the Beijing Declaration and Platform for Action[133] (Beijing+10 Review) in March 2005, including narrowing gender gaps in education and health, women's greater participation in the workforce and in decision-making, and a greater number of "focal points for women or gender equality in government offices".[134] However, "this review called attention to the many areas where women's equality is still not a reality – continuing high rates of violence against women in all parts of the world including in armed conflict, increasing incidence of HIV/AIDS among women, gender inequality in employment, lack of sexual and reproductive health rights and a lack of equal access under the law to land and property".[135]

A range of other groups in society" are vulnerable to human rights violations by virtue of their status, their difference or their exclusion from power. Ultimately the test of success of a human rights based approach is the extent to which it encompasses and addresses as priorities the human rights of such groups.

9.2 Experience in Ireland

The history of discrimination and treatment of vulnerable groups in Ireland is well documented. Women were traditionally excluded from decision-making in private, political and commercial life – captured by Article 41.2 of the Constitution regarding their role in the home. Even today, on average, Irish women earn 85 per cent of their male counterpart's pay for doing work of equal value. This disparity widens for women with higher education qualifications. While progress has been made in the boardrooms of the commercial sphere and commitments have been made with regard to state bodies,[136] women represent a mere 13 per cent of TDs in the Dáil and 15 per cent of elected councillors - despite women making up 51 per cent of the population.

Beyond numbers, a range of steps have been taken in terms of policies, legislation and institutions to address an acknowledged problem of discrimination and vulnerable groups – in many cases after sustained campaigning by civil society organizations. Legislative progress includes the Employment Equality Act, Equal Status Act and Prohibition of Incitement to Hatred Act, although these have not been without criticism for their deficiencies.[137] More recent legislation undermines some of these protections.[138]

Recent economic success in Ireland has seen general improvement in social and economic conditions. Many who, in the past, would have been forced to emigrate now have the opportunity to live in their own country. Many who were economically disadvantaged have the opportunity to work. The economic boom has the potential to generate tax revenue for the

State to fund social reform, etc., but Ireland continues to have the lowest tax take in the EU.[139]

Even those who are literate, educated or economically independent may still struggle to assert their human rights. Education or wealth may not protect migrants, people with disabilities, women, etc., from discrimination. However, poverty remains the most prevalent common denominator among vulnerable groups and those most likely to face discrimination in Ireland. Despite Ireland's economic revival, poverty remains a central problem. Ireland has the most unequal distribution of income in the EU, with the richest 10 per cent of the population having 14 times more wealth than the poorest 10 per cent.[140] Despite being ranked eighth in the world on the UN Human Development Index, and the second wealthiest country in the world, Ireland has the third highest level of human poverty in 18 industrialised OECD countries reviewed in the UN Human Development Report 2005.[141]

Ireland has among the highest rates of child poverty in Europe with children up to 50 per cent more likely to be in poverty than adults. In a UN league table of child poverty published in 2000, Ireland was found to have the sixth highest percentage of children living in income poverty amongst twenty-three OECD countries, with 8 per cent of Irish children experiencing severe or consistent poverty.[142] The ESRI *Report on Gender Equality* 2005 highlighted the fact that 23 per cent of Ireland's female population are at risk of poverty. The stark reality of poverty is illustrated by the case made for a national survey of nutrition by the St. Vincent de Paul Society, based on its need to spend a third of its budget on providing food.[143] Comprehensive data on matters such as nutrition is regarded as a basic starting point in any overseas developing country serious about combating poverty – yet, it is does not appear to be available in Ireland.

A recent *Quality of Life in Ireland*[144] survey found most Irish people to be happy with their quality of life. The 10 per cent who do not share this view are largely made up of elderly and disadvantaged socio-economic groups. The "poverty factor" means that identifying who are discriminated against and who are vulnerable in Ireland today is, on one level, straightforward. *Building an Inclusive Society*, the 2002 review of the National Anti-Poverty Strategy under the Programme for Prosperity and Fairness, listed women, children and young people, older people, people with disabilities, migrants and ethnic minorities as particularly vulnerable groups. Within some vulnerable groups there are sub-groups at even greater risk, such as Traveller children, or victims of trafficking as a sub-group of migrant women. The groups identified as vulnerable represent a significant proportion of the population. For example, 270,000 people have a disability or suffer from a long-term health problem; 400,000 or over 10 per cent of the population are aged over 65 and, of these, over a quarter live alone; 1,200 Travellers live in halting sites; 48,000 households are in need of social housing and 5,500 households are homeless; 10 per cent of the population were born outside the country. In addition, vulnerability is not confined to minority status, e.g. women represent the majority of the population.

As highlighted by a 2002 NESC Report, the nature of Ireland's vulnerable groups is also subject to change.[145] Those outside the labour force (principally in home duties or retired) have replaced the unemployed as the most typically poor category. Similarly, new vulnerable groups also arise, such as asylum-seekers denied the right to work and receiving direct provision instead of welfare payments. The 2004 Annual Report of the Equality Authority confirms the persistence of racial discrimination, reflected in the fact that "race" and Traveller grounds continue to comprise the majority of complaints to that body.

"Ireland is amongst the most unequal countries in the EU, with one of the highest rates of relative income poverty."

Combat Poverty Agency, *An analysis of the distributive and poverty impacts of Budget 2002*

The 2002 NESC report also pointed out the vulnerability of those economic migrants from EU states who arrive in Ireland lacking the connections or language skills to secure work. Media reports, trade unions and NGOs such as the Immigrant Council of Ireland all confirm widespread abuse of migrant workers' human rights, and poor state investigation of their ill-treatment. The 2004 US State Department Report on Human Rights in Ireland observes: "Societal discrimination and racial violence against immigrants and ethnic minorities, such as Asians and Africans continued to be a growing problem. Racially motivated incidents involved physical violence, intimidation, and verbal slurs, and the majority of incidents of racist violence took place in public places." Yet, in 2002 the Government estimated that in order to meet the targets set out in the National Development Plan, 340,000 migrant workers would be needed by 2006. It is therefore somewhat ironic that despite the increasing recognition of the importance of migrant workers to the economy, they are also at risk. This illustrates the economic imperative of acting on HRBA, including the 2005 recommendations of the UN Committee on the Elimination of Racial Discrimination regarding work permits in Ireland. The current situation has been described by former President Mary Robinson as "frighteningly resembling bonded servitude".[146]

Steps taken, such as State workplace initiatives,[147] information hotlines and the National Action Plan Against Racism,[148] are open to criticism for not being integrated or strategic – indeed being contradicted by other Government programmes, policies and attitudes. It is unfortunate that Ireland has refused to become a party to the International Convention on the Protection of the Rights of All Migrant Workers and Members of Their Families.

This evolving nature of vulnerability in Irish society highlights the need for ongoing review and properly disaggregated data. A 2005 report, *Inclusion is Everyone's Business*, highlighted the fact that levels of deprivation in Dublin have worsened over the 11 years up to 2002.[149] It noted a "lack of detailed data in relation to poverty and social inclusion" and a "hidden" disadvantaged group of those in the private rented sector. The State has also been criticized by a range of international bodies for its failure to systematically collate disaggregated data to track the prohibited grounds of discrimination in Ireland's treaty obligations. The circumstances of specific vulnerable groups are also underexplored - for example, the UN CEDAW Committee, in its 2005 report on Ireland, expressed its concern at "the lack of information on the extent of the problem" of trafficking in women and girls into Ireland.

Womens' Rights demonstration in Dublin
© *Eamon Farrell/Photocall Ireland*

Conclusion

▨ Development processes, institutions, etc., in Ireland fail to systematically review and address the discrimination prohibited by international treaties or prioritise the protection of vulnerable groups – nor is there accountability for failing to do so.

Official data is not uniformly disaggregated by sex, age, ethnicity, etc., with major gaps in the availability, and use, of such data in Ireland's development planning.

The failure to systematically address discrimination and prioritise vulnerable groups is not addressed by effective accountability for political and administrative policy choices, maladministration, etc. (see accountability below).

Endnotes

133. Beijing Declaration and Platform for Action adopted at the Fourth World Conference on Women, held in Beijing in 1995.

134. Review of the implementation of the Beijing Platform for Action and the outcome documents of the special session of the General Assembly entitled "Women 2000: gender equality, development and peace for the twenty-first century", Report of the Secretary-General, E/CN.6/2005/2. See generally www.un.org/womenwatch/daw/Review.

135. "Governments pledge to accelerate efforts to achieve equality for women and fulfil Beijing commitments, as UN Commission concludes", press release, UN Department of Public Information, DPI/2383F, March 2005.

136. "State Boards told to be 40% female", *Irish Times*, 22 April 2005. Instruction to all State Boards by Minister Frank Fahey, Minister of State responsible for equality.

137. In the case of the Equality Act, 2004, differential treatment is permitted in the case of non-EU nationals with regard to access to education and state services, as is discrimination on the basis of nationality in the area of immigration and residency.

138. The Social Welfare (Miscellaneous Provisions) Act, 2004 and the Residential Tenancies Act, 2004 exclude same sex couples from protection from discrimination against cohabiting.

139. CORI, *Ireland's tax take among the lowest in Europe*, www.cori.ie/justice/publications/briefing/taxation/page2.htm

140. *Socio-Economic Review 2005: Pathways to Inclusion* (2005), CORI Justice Commission, based on 2003 figures from the *EU Survey on Income and Living Conditions* (2005), Central Statistics Office. The UN Human Development Report 2005 found a factor of 9.7 times, based on 1996 data. While it has increased in real terms, Ireland continues to have the lowest social protection expenditure (encompassing the right to health, housing, disability) by GDP in the European Union. While consistent poverty is in decline, relative poverty is on the increase.

141. *UN Human Development Report 2005* (hdr.undp.org/reports/global/2005/pdf/HDR05_complete.pdf). The Human Development Index covers three dimensions of human welfare: income, education and health. Its purpose is not to give a complete picture of human development but to provide a measure that goes beyond income. Wealth is measured in this report as per capita GDP. The human poverty index reflects deprivations in four dimensions: vulnerability to death at a relatively early age; exclusion from knowledge; the percentage of people living below the income poverty line (50% of the median adjusted household disposable income); and social exclusion as measured by the rate of long-term unemployment (12 months or more).

142. *A League Table of Child Poverty in Rich Nations*, UNICEF / UNICEF Innocenti Research Centre (2000)

143. Part III: Consultation with the Non-Governmental Organisation Sector, *International Covenant on Economic, Social and Cultural Rights: Second Report by Ireland* (2000).

144. Amárach Consulting survey for Guinness Ireland, 2005.

145. *NESC Report 110 - An Investment in Quality: Services, Inclusion and Enterprise*, National Economic and Social Council, Department of an Taoiseach.

146. Addressing Immigrant Council of Ireland conference, 'Immigration Irelands Future', 11 December 2004.

147. E.g. Dublin Bus, *Equality and Diversity Action Plan* (2003-2006).

148. www.nccri.com/action-plan.html

149. Social Inclusion Unit of Dublin City Council.

"The prisons are full of victims. It's the planners who should be in jail. They put people to live in areas with no transport, no community services – sometimes even without a shop. What do they expect?"

Suzanne Power, Journalist, RTÉ Radio 1, 19th July 2005

"Resigning is a dirty
word in Irish politics and
it is long past time for a
change in attitude"

Stephen Collins, *Sunday
Tribune,* **5th May 2005**

10.1 Definitions and core principles

The core HRBA principle of accountability refers to accountability for human rights impact. Accountability is a composite human right involving rights to due process, to effective remedies, to equal treatment, etc. While it is not exclusively about prosecution or punishment, some circumstances may require this. Generally, this principle includes accountability for transparent decision-making, clarity around, and awareness of, the responsibilities of those involved as duty-bearers or rights-holders. It requires human rights based benchmarks by which progress is measured, as well as reward and sanction for success and failure in achieving positive human rights impact.

"An accountability procedure depends on, but goes beyond, monitoring. It is a mechanism or device by which duty-bearers are answerable for their acts or omissions in relation to their duties. An accountability procedure provides right-holders with an opportunity to understand how duty-bearers have discharged, or failed to discharge, their obligations, and it also provides duty-bearers with an opportunity to explain their conduct. While accountability implies some form of remedy and reparation, it does not necessarily imply punishment. ...

Broadly speaking, there are four categories of accountability mechanism:
- Judicial, e.g. judicial review of executive acts and omissions;
- Quasi-judicial, e.g. Ombuds institutions, international human rights Treaty-bodies;
- Administrative, e.g. the preparation, publication and scrutiny of human rights impact assessments;
- Political, e.g. parliamentary processes."

United Nations High Commission for Human Rights, *Draft Guidelines: A Human Rights Approach to Poverty Reduction Strategies* **(2002)**

*Kathy Sinnott MEP outside
Leinster House when a
Seanad candidate.*
© *Bryan O'Brien/Irish Times*

Accountability therefore encompasses political, as well as administrative, decision-making. It includes accountability for both process (how the decision was made) and result (who gains/loses in human rights terms from the policy/practice). Where special responsibilities, privileges and powers are granted to particular individuals and institutions, they must be matched by appropriate levels of accountability. In the shift from welfare/charity to a human rights framework, empowerment and participation, described above, are fundamental requirements to ensure accountability; and where these are absent or inadequate, impunity prevails. The HRBA principle of accountability is one of the defining features of a State which applies the rule of law.

A key aspect of accountability is effective legal incorporation of Ireland's international commitments so that remedies are available on the national level. This is required by the treaties themselves, and is discussed in chapter 5 above.

A major opportunity to ensure effectiveness of such national remedies is through reform of public administration. The UNDP concept of public administration encompasses the machinery of the State and as well as its management:

"The *aggregate machinery* (policies, rules, procedures, systems, organizational structures, personnel, etc.) funded by the State budget and in charge of the management and direction of the affairs of the executive government, and its interaction with other stakeholders in the State, society and external environment.

The *management* and implementation of the whole set of government activities dealing with the implementation of laws, regulations and decisions of the government and the management related to the provision of public services."[150]

Key components of HRBA can only be achieved with the aid, inter alia, of an effective public administration that is accountable for its performance. This requires review of organizational structures, decentralisation, personnel management, public finance, results-based management and regulatory reforms – not limited to criteria such as value for money but to a holistic assessment of human rights impact.

Crucially, such reform needs to develop not only the capacities of rights holders to claim and exercise their rights, but also of duty bearers to fulfil human rights obligations. For example, it increases the pressure on the public administration to put disadvantaged and vulnerable groups at the core of policy and of development strategies – while ensuring that the administration is allocated the resources, builds the capacity, and is held accountable, to deliver. The application of this core principle ensures development that is relevant, effective and efficient while achieving greater impact and sustainability as outlined in Table 2.

This is recognised by the evolution of the term "good governance" in the UN system to describe the need to apply HRBA to assess the performance of state institutions, policies, programmes, budget processes and choices - the basis of sustainable human development. In the last decade in particular, anti-corruption and transparency have been understood to be central to development. Ireland expresses strong support for this aspect of HRBA in its overseas development programmes. The following section examines the extent to which it applies this principle at home.

10.2 Experience in Ireland

Ireland has a complex web of mechanisms aimed at ensuring different forms of accountability - political, financial, legal, etc. These include state mechanisms and institutions such as the courts, ad hoc Tribunals of Inquiry, Civil Service and Local Appointments Commission, Ombudsman, Public Offices Commission, Information Commissioner, Office of the Attorney General, Office of the Director of Public Prosecutions,[151] Local Government Audit Service, Comptroller and Auditor General, Local Authority Audit Service, Garda Síochána, Employment Appeals Tribunal, Equality Tribunal, Equality Authority, Director for Corporate Enforcement and so forth.[152] Civil society actors - the media in particular - also have a fundamental role to play in ensuring accountability.

"The operations within government departments and within state-sponsored bodies are almost entirely closed to public scrutiny. We know about what goes on within them only in so far as a conscious decision is taken to publish a decision or report, often presented as a remarkable act of magnanimity on the part of the body concerned."

Barrington, *The Irish Administrative System* (1980)

"Corruption is the antithesis of republicanism. Political corruption is the subordination of a public interest to private interest. Its purpose is mirrored in its means of operation. It is carried out beyond public scrutiny as a set of private understandings. But it also requires a corrosion of the idea of public interest itself. Political decisions that are made for private reasons to favour those who favour the politicians have to be justified by an invented set of public policies..."

Fintan O'Toole, Thomas Davis Lecture "The Unreal Republic", RTE Radio 1, 12th May 2005

Protestors outside the Fianna Fáil hospitality tent at the Galway races in June 2005.

Political accountability to the electorate is frequently highlighted as the ultimate point of reference for accountability. In the case of socio-economic rights, it is presented by some politicians as if it is an alternative to justiciability. In principle, the State's preferred electoral system of proportional representation is conducive to meeting key principles of HRBA, for instance, through localised engagement with elected representatives and representation of minority voices in national decision-making. However, a by-product of this system, has been its negative impact on the coherence of planning at national level and on collective accountability for policy choices of the Government. The notion of accountability to the population as a whole, and to vulnerable groups in particular, is widely seen as trumped by the imperative for politicians to get re-elected. Rivalry (even between members of the same party) is fuelled by multi-seat constituencies as well as the close-knit nature of Irish society. This has historically reduced much political activity to writing letters in support of a constituent's medical card or civil service job application. At Government level this manifests itself in the need to "look after" marginal constituencies. The process and basis for the recent decentralisation programme is illustrative of these features. The lack of consultation with those expected to relocate has been highlighted by their representative bodies. Media coverage of the decentralisation debate spoke of towns winning and losing according to the power of their local representatives. In addition to questions about the process, a range of human rights concerns also arises as regards the impact on efficiency and advocacy of decentralisation such as Development Cooperation Ireland and the Equality Authority being moved to Limerick and Roscrea respectively.

Demographic and other changes may be impacting on some historical features of the Irish political system. The impact of the political corruption unveiled in recent times on wider society in terms of lost funding for the right to health, education, etc., is not highlighted by political leaders, nor is accountability effectively demanded by the public. This flows in part from low public awareness and lack of empowerment discussed above. A sense of political welfarism is fuelled by access to influence, development and funding being seen as matters of political largesse – rather than rights based on transparent, rational development planning in the *national* interest.

A key institution in the state system for ensuring criminal accountability, is An Garda Síochána. To this end, it has been granted privileges and powers which must be accompanied by appropriate levels of accountability. This needs to be read in light of an Irish Times-MRBI poll published in February 2003, which found that 37 per cent of electoral voters had no confidence in the fairness of the Gardaí, rising in the 18-24 age group to 54 per cent. A catalogue of potentially criminal behaviour by Gardaí has been exposed – accompanied by evidence of cover-up to avoid accountability. This ranges from removing identity numbers when policing public protests in May 2002, to the Morris Tribunal's findings of cover-up by members of the service and other behaviour described as "scandalous" by the investigating judge.[153] A number of highly publicised cases have required public apologies by the State and awards of compensation against Gardaí. In its latest report, the European Committee for the Prevention of Torture expressed concern about credible reports of ill-treatment by members of an Garda Síochána.[154] A 2005 human rights audit by An Garda Síochána itself identified the need for an impact assessment of existing and future policies and the need for support for members in reporting human rights abuses.[155] To this might be added the need for sanction for failure to report such abuses. In this context, doubts have been widely expressed regarding the adequacy of the design of the new Garda Ombudsman Commission proposed in the Garda Síochána Bill, 2004, to succeed the Garda Complaints Board. In addition, the Irish Human Rights Commission has concluded that an independent complaints mechanism is "only one part of a broader programme of police reform", and "that the vesting of oversight and appointment functions with an independent and representative agency, such as a Police Authority as recommended by the Patten Report, could make a valuable contribution to the promotion of human rights within Irish policing".[156]

The costs of lack of effective performance accountability in Ireland are incalculable. As just one example, Amnesty International reports that one in five women in Ireland has experienced systematic violence at the hands of a partner, but that:

"There is little monitoring of the effectiveness of legal and other measures to prevent, identify, investigate and punish this violence. Clear channels of accountability have not been created for the Government or its agents- the Gardai are the only statutory agency with a formal policy on domestic violence, for example. Yet, even its implementation has not been reviewed."[157]

It is in this kind of context that justiciability as a key element in ensuring accountability needs to be noted. In its 1999 submission to the CESCR, the Irish Commission for Justice and Peace and the Council for Social Welfare put the case for justiciable socio-economic rights as a means of ensuring accountability:

"If social and economic rights are to be enforceable, responsibilities have to be identified, implementation consistently monitored and policies and programmes continuously evaluated. By making them justiciable, rights hitherto broadly expressed would be increasingly specified in assessable quantifiable and qualitative terms. The whole legal, political and economic system would *ipso facto* become more orientated to specificity of performance and accountability. Programmes would be more accurately targeted, evaluation and monitoring more effective and the real needs of those most in need brought more to the forefront."[158]

In addition, the principle of accountability requires examination of the State's direct actions and omissions, as well as of the functions it delegates, such as through privatisation. Thus, when the State chooses to place children in the care of religious bodies or when it contracts private companies to transport prisoners, deport migrants, etc., HRBA requires that it be accountable to the rights-holders concerned.

As noted by an NGO Shadow Report submitted to the UN Committee on the Elimination of Racial Discrimination (CERD) in 2004, the fact that "the vast majority of Irish schools remain under the ownership and management of the Catholic Church [is] due to the State's abrogation of its responsibility to develop an inclusive state system of primary education".[159] Another such Shadow Report highlights one of the consequences of this abrogation, by citing a letter issued to Catholic primary schools in Dublin advising them "to draw up enrolment policies that clearly state that non-Catholic children can only be accepted if there are vacancies left unfilled by Catholics".[160] In the same vein, a state-established body on racism notes that Muslim children sit at the back of the class or play in the corridor while the rest are being taught religion.[161] Thus, while individuals and non-state actors also have duties and

"The Committee notes with regret that, despite its previous recommendation in 1999, no steps have been taken to incorporate or reflect the Covenant in domestic legislation, and that the State party could not provide information on case law in which the Covenant and its rights were invoked before the courts."

UN Committee on Economic, Social and Cultural Rights, 2002 concluding observations on Ireland's second periodic report

An Taoiseach with pupils from Belvedere College, taking part in a 48 hour sleep out and 24 hour fast, outside the Bank of Ireland, College Green, to raise funds for Focus Ireland, The Arrupe Society, and The Los Angeles Society.

© Eric Luke/Irish Times

responsibilities for the human rights of others, the primary focus of HRBA remains the State. It is the party bound by its treaty commitments to regulate the behaviour of others.

Accountability (in particular for socio-economic rights) faces specific challenges in a globalised world. State functions are increasingly privatised or delegated, and economic actors are increasingly linked with complex international structures. Thus, making the connection between the State's human rights treaty obligations and the range of non-state forces that impact on daily life is increasingly acknowledged. It remains the case that, for accountability purposes, the State remains the primary duty-holder. As the Minister of State at the Department of Foreign Affairs recently told the UN Commission on Human Rights:

> "It is true that international human rights law places legal obligations on States and that States have, and should continue to have, the primary responsibility for the promotion and protection of human rights. At the same time, it is important that businesses are conscious of the effects of their actions on people. They must be, where necessary, obliged to ensure that their actions conform to certain standards."[162]

United Nations business expert David Weissbrodt at a press conference in Dublin with Colm Ó Cuanacháin Secretary General of Amnesty International's Irish Section.Mr Weissbrodt was in Dublin challenging the Irish Government and the business community to meet their obligations to protect human rights and push for a UN Working Group to address the responsibilities of transnational corporations.

© *Leon Farrell/Photocall Ireland*

Ireland was one of a group of States which requested, for the first time, that the UN High Commissioner for Human Rights report formally to them on the human rights responsibilities of private economic entities.[163]

Initiatives in Ireland on corporate social responsibility include the Foundation for Investing in Communities established in 1998 to support businesses in adopting socially responsible policies and practices. In the same way that a tax clearance certificate is a prerequisite for many State grants and contracts, the need for a form of "human rights" clearance system for public contracts is also highlighted by the ongoing Gama Construction saga.[164] What is needed is a clear signal by Ireland that it only welcomes international investment which respects workers' rights, including, for example, the right of workers to organise. An adequately resourced and effective Labour Inspectorate is necessary if accountability for human rights obligations in that sector is to be delivered.[165]

The media (as part of civil society) has a key role in helping to apply this principle of human right based approaches. It both benefits from the guarantees of human rights (notably freedom of expression) and has the power to impact on human rights more generally (positively and negatively). Human rights based approaches review both the nature of State regulation of the media and the media's own human rights responsibilities and freedoms. For example, Ray Burke TD, as Minister for Communications, was found by the interim report of the Flood Tribunal in 2002 to have unacceptably promoted the interests of Century Radio at the expense of the national broadcaster, RTÉ, in 1989, receiving bribes in the process. While he was eventually investigated by the Tribunal, and later convicted by the courts – and the Standards in Public Office Commission was subsequently established – it took over a decade for this political interference to be exposed, highlighting the importance of effective systems to ensure media independence.

Our Rights, Our Future

Linked to the role of the media in ensuring accountability in public life, is the role of whistle-blowers, who expose malpractice and corruption, whether in State administration or the private sector.[166] A number of attempts to legislate in Ireland for such protection have failed, despite recent examples of people risking their careers to legitimately expose corruption and other practices antithetical to human rights. The fact that planning corruption was widely acknowledged as taking place, but only exposed when two private individuals offered a reward for information in a newspaper advertisement highlights a problem with the planning process as well as the range of accountability mechanisms responsible for corruption.

In terms of ensuring accountability for human rights impact, the Irish Human Rights Commission in principle has a key role. An Taoiseach has stated that:

> "In formulating the legislation it was my intention that the Commission would be a model for others to follow, and one that would set rather than follow standards of best international practice in this area".[167]

International standards for national human rights institutions require minimum guarantees of independence and transparency in the appointment process; adequate and stable resources to carry out their extensive mandates; and, not surprisingly, that the institution apply the international human rights framework to their work.[168] This specifically requires that the Irish Human Rights Commission act to address Ireland's failure to incorporate, and to comply with, its economic and social rights obligations. More broadly, it requires that the Commission address Ireland's obligation to apply HRBA in its development.

Effective application of HRBA in Ireland requires the Irish Human Rights Commission to play a key role. As the national human rights institution it is the body in Ireland already tasked with ensuring HRBA is applied. The extent to which it is ready for the task raises questions of its visibility, resources and capacity. It also raises questions regarding the extent to which policy-makers and institutions at all levels acknowledge its legitimate role across all aspects of national development.

Overall, in spite of the plethora of accountability institutions and (or perhaps because of) the electoral process, public confidence in the accountability of public institutions is low. In a MORI Ireland 2004 opinion poll, *Trust in Public Institutions*, 65 per cent of those surveyed did not believe that public sector organizations are open and honest about mistakes. "Taking responsibility for mistakes" was identified as one of the key factors in people's confidence in institutions.

Protesters outside Namhi Disability conference in Dublin.
© *Gareth Chaney/Photocall Ireland*

The recent spate of tribunals is identified as a factor in popular trust in national institutions. However, the MORI survey does not address whether this is a reduction in popular trust from a pre-existing high level – or whether the reduction is due to lack of confidence in the tribunals' capacity to ensure accountability. However, tribunals may well be confirming rather than unveiling behaviour for the public. The new focus on corruption as a specific challenge to

> "If the Irish Human Rights Commission does all that it has set itself, it has the capacity to transform many practices in public life. It may also face hostility from those who have been content that Ireland has a paper commitment to various human rights instruments, but that these matter little in practice"
>
> *Irish Times* **Editorial, 1st April 2003**

accountability, has seen Transparency International, an international NGO specialising in issues of corruption, establish an Irish office in 2004. Its reason for doing so is the "enduring public cynicism towards political and commercial actors and systems".[169]

Human rights based accountability requires that relevant policy commitments are bolstered by clear standards by which performance is measured and accountability ensured, including, where necessary, by legal enforcement. The resources and time allocated by the State to reporting to UN treaty bodies reflects acknowledgment of accountability at a diplomatic level. What is clearly needed is an equivalent respect for domestic accountability mechanisms.

A recommended starting point is an economic analysis of the costs to Ireland of the failure to apply the HRBA. For example, the cost of ineffectual accountability mechanisms for issues ranging from discarded electronic voting machines to illegal nursing home charges; from corrupt payments or non-transparent settlement of child abuse claims with religious orders; the cost arising from failure to address the root causes of crime or rehabilitate offenders, etc. Cost analyses such as these are needed to inform debate by demonstrating the economic case in favour of HRBA, and the key role of accountability in this regard.

Conclusion

- There is no systematic commitment or procedure to apply full spectrum human rights impact assessment to all laws, plans, proposals, policies, budgets and programmes.
- Human rights standards are not translated into benchmarks for measuring progress and enhancing accountability.
- Ireland has not systematically developed adequate laws, policies, institutions, administrative procedures, and mechanisms of redress and accountability that ensure delivery on entitlements, respond to denial and violations of rights, and ensure accountability.
- Particularly in the case of economic and social rights, Ireland has failed to identify positive obligations of duty-holders (to protect, promote and provide) and negative obligations (to abstain from violations) of the relevant actors, including local authorities, state agencies, etc.

Endnotes

150. UNDP Practice Note on Public Administration Reform.
151. www.dppireland.ie
152. A compendium of avenues for redress and complaint for consumers and service users is provided in *Where to Complain*, Comhairle (2004).
153. www.morristribunal.ie
154. Report to the Government of Ireland on the visit to Ireland carried out by the European Committee for the Prevention of Torture and Inhuman or Degrading Treatment or Punishment (CPT) from 20 to 28 May 2002, CPT/Inf (2003) 36, published September 2003.
155. *An Garda Síochána Human Rights Audit: A report from Ionann Management Consultants*, An Garda Síochána (2004).
156. "Human Rights Commission gives broad welcome to amendments in Garda Bill 2004", Press Release, 1 March 2004.
157. *Justice and Accountability: Stop Violence against Women*, Amnesty International (Irish Section) (2005).
158. *Completing the circle: making good the UN human rights monitoring system at national level: the case of Ireland* (1999).
159. www.statewatch.org/news/ 2005/jan/ireland-ngo-alliance.pdf
160. *Shadow Report on The First National Report to the UN Committee on the Convention on the Elimination of All Forms of Racial Discrimination*, Educate Together (2005).

161. Philip Watt, Director of the National Consultative Council on Racism and Interculturalism, Irish Times newspaper, 12 April 2005.

162. High Level Statement from Ireland, Statement by Mr Conor Lenihan TD Minister of State at the Department of Foreign Affairs with special responsibility for Overseas Development and Human Rights, UN Commission on Human Rights, Geneva, 17 March 2005.

163. At the UN Commission on Human Rights in Geneva, 2004. This followed years of international work on Norms on the Responsibilities of Transnational Corporations and other Business Enterprises with Regard to Human Rights. These norms were adopted by the United Nations Sub-Commission on the Promotion and Protection of Human Rights and have seen a range of companies adjust their practices and polices to meet the standards they contain. See Amnesty International, The UN Human Rights Norms for Business: Towards Legal Accountability (AI Index: IOR 42/001/2004).

164. The fact that GAMA Construction has Corporate Governance rules and a Corporate Governance and Audit Committees cautions against undue confidence in non-enforceable statements of principles or the mere existence of oversight mechanisms. (www.holding.gama.com.tr)

165. As of April 2005 the Inspectorate had a total of 21 inspectors with the number of workplace inspections and prosecutions falling in recent years.

166. OECD Policy Brief, Building Public Trust: Ethics Measures in OECD Countries, www.oecd.org/dataoecd/60/43/1899427.pdf

167. Quoted in the Irish Human Rights Commission's first Strategic Plan, Promoting and Protecting Human Rights In Irish Society: A Plan for 2003-2006 (2003).

168. Principles relating to the status and functioning of national institutions for protection and promotion of human rights (Paris Principles), endorsed by the UN Commission on Human Rights in March 1992 (resolution 1992/54) and by the UN General Assembly (resolution A/RES/48/134) in December 1993.

169. www.transparency.ie/about_ti/default.htm

> "The main issue is whether one has a rights-based template. I do not believe we, in the political theatre, have had a proper informed debate about that. The simplistic response has always been to do whatever the rights-based approach suggests without looking at the consequences or the implications for the roll-out and the targeting of services or at who should get what. ..."
>
> **Minister for Health and Children, Micheál Martin TD, Dáil Éireann, 12th February 2003**

11.1 Introduction

The desire to entrench human rights principles of democracy, openness and accountability is recognised not only as important for the well-being of individuals and communities, but also as essential components of equitable economic and social progress and sustainable development. Worldwide, there is a growing conviction that the implementation of HRBA principles strengthens social harmony and cohesion, advances the process of genuine development, and promotes the accountability and legitimacy of governments. The global popular movement that underpins these developments has been inspired by the human rights principles and standards enshrined in instruments and resolutions developed by the United Nations. International organizations including international financial institutions recognize that achieving long-term economic and other goals is dependent on openness, democratic systems of government, accountability, an active civil society and respect for the rule of law.

Domestically, Ireland has followed a vision of development that has resulted in the disadvantaged and vulnerable being marginalised, and has prioritised the needs of those who already have access to power and influence. In large part, the status quo is maintained because the five core principles at the heart of human rights based approaches are not effectively applied across key policy choices and decision-making procedures. Many challenges to implementing HRBA in less economically developed countries are also much in evidence in Ireland. These include:

Weak public awareness of the full spectrum of human rights – and what they mean for development choices being made.
Far from fulfilling their legal obligations to systematically inform the public regarding the nature and scope of Ireland's international human rights obligations, political leaders often mislead and obfuscate.[170] Not surprisingly, there is little or no informed debate regarding the direction of Ireland's development and little organised public demand that human rights be the means and the goal for Ireland's development. The Irish public has had little effective opportunity to state their view on key issues such as the incorporation of economic and social rights into Irish law. Similarly, lack of confidence in the integrity and accountability of public institutions leads to cynicism and apathy even when there are genuine opportunities to participate and influence. This is a fundamental challenge for advocates for change in Irish society.

Therefore, weak capacity for HRBA programming
In a negative cycle, weak public demand for human rights based development has contributed to a situation where it is not politically prioritised. In this context, there is little technical capacity in the public service to make human rights operational through planning and programming processes, budget allocations, etc. Leadership and technical expertise is needed to ensure conceptual clarity and coherence in policy and programming tools.[171] Without such guidelines and tools the vicious cycle is perpetuated. Civil servants and other advisers are not empowered to ensure that political decision-makers are presented with human rights based approaches to apply. Such reviews and assessments as do exist fail to encompass accountability for human rights based process and outcomes.

The Human Rights Commission is mandated by statute to ensure HRBA is applied to Ireland's development processes. However, it continues to suffer from insufficient resources and political backing to effectively prioritise this.

The key recommendations outlined in the table below are for **human rights based development promoted through a National Human Rights Action Plan (NHRAP)**. While steps towards a NHRAP are outlined below, and such a plan would be the ideal vehicle for promoting HRBA, these steps pertain notwithstanding any absence of political commitment to a NHRAP, and are set out here as components and processes that can and should be achieved independently of such a plan. These recommendations will require considerable planning and resources from civil society, as well by state institutions. A decision to use human rights as the litmus test for a State's success goes beyond questions of law – it indicates the kind of state and the kind of society, the people of Ireland choose to have.

Are the institutions and procedures that impact on my life based on human rights? Questions I might ask:

▨ Am I treated as a drain on resources, a victim in need of charity or as a rights-holder?

▨ Are the procedures, offices, forms etc, I encounter accessible and user-friendly?

▨ Am I consulted on issues that impact on my life? Am I able to participate in decision-making processes?

▨ Are any factors that make me vulnerable acknowledged and treated as a priority?

▨ Am I confident that someone will be held accountable if my entitlements are not met? Is there a process for holding duty-holders to account?

"Try to imagine a little African country, somewhere in the middle of that great continent. From everything we've heard and read about it, it fits all the stereotypes. A governing party that masquerades as democratic, but rumours of political corruption have been established time and again to be true. Members of the government all have big houses and drive flashy cars, even though they are surrounded by poverty."

Fergus Finlay in "If Ireland were in Africa, we'd send in observers to help build democracy", *The Irish Examiner*, **17th February 2004**

Children from Tallaght at a photocall, Merrion Hotel, Dublin, to support the Wella International Womens' Day Lunch in aid of An Cosan, an organisation which promotes the philosophy that education is key to eradicating poverty.
© *Photocall Ireland*

Key recommendations towards HRBA

1. A human rights based approach to Ireland's development

To advance progress towards development based on HRBA in Ireland, a National Human Rights Action Plan is recommended. With a realistic date by which it would be achieved, immediate attention should focus on the process of informing public opinion and increasing effective public demand for human rights based development in Ireland. As noted throughout, this process is as important as the outcomes expected.

While the steps outlined below can be undertaken without necessarily adopting a NHRAP, a NHRAP can provide a unifying vision to maximize coherence and mutual reinforcement of efforts by civil society and others. It would allow Ireland to learn from the experience of others and draw support from the UN and others.

2. Steps towards a National Human Rights Action Plan

▨ Coordinate disparate voices into a broad-based human rights movement including "traditional" human rights actors, media, faith-based organizations, trade unions, etc.

▨ Incorporate Ireland's human rights treaty obligations through a Constitutional amendment[172] and become a party to outstanding human rights treaties, e.g. the Migrant Workers Convention.

▨ Strengthen the Irish Human Rights Commission to become a catalyst promoting HRBA discussed in this report (for example providing economic analysis of the costs of adopting and not adopting HRBA).

▨ Actively apply the rich body of lessons from other countries to inform a truly effective NHRAP in Ireland.

▨ Implement a national programme of human rights education and awareness-raising through formal/informal education, full integration in schools curricula, media debate, etc.

Expected outcomes

The strengths of HRBA include:

▨ Legitimacy and clarity deriving from development based explicitly on human rights recognised in international law.

▨ Accountability deriving from duties and duty-bearers in the development process – as part of a shift from a charity focus to one of rights and obligations.

▨ Enhanced relevance and sustainability deriving from free, meaningful and active participation of all people in their development.

▨ Enhanced coherence across sectors (e.g. health, education environment) as HRBA works to address the inter-linked issues systematically and strategically.

▨ Enhanced protection for individuals and communities from unintentional harm in development processes, as well as prioritisation of the most vulnerable.

▨ Enhanced civil society coordination and coherence as regards human rights norms and methodologies applicable to development in Ireland with appropriate interaction with State institutions.

▨ A comprehensive assessment of human rights needs; informed public debate aimed at ensuring political commitment which accords with legal obligations.

▨ Guidance provided to government officials, non-governmental organizations (NGOs), professional groups, educators, advocates and other members of civil society regarding the steps necessary to ensure that human rights are vindicated.

▨ Concrete initiatives identified, achievable targets set, linkages with other national programmes established and lessons learned from other contexts where HRBA is applied.

▨ More sound public administration, stronger rule of law, economic performance enhanced by human rights based approaches.

▨ Concerns of vulnerable groups more effectively addressed through a comprehensive approach emphasising prevention.

▨ A society-wide, non-confrontational consideration of human rights issues promoted.

11.2 A National Human Rights Action Plan for Ireland

The concept of a National Human Rights Action Plan (NHRAP) recognizes that no country has a perfect human rights record. The nature of human rights shortcomings will inevitably vary, but every member of the international community must take substantive action if the promise of the Charter of the United Nations to "promote social progress and better standards of life in larger freedom" is to be made a reality.

The basic idea endorsed by the 1993 Vienna World Conference was that each country would recognize that it faces challenges to improve its human rights observance – it would entail starting from its current situation, whatever that might be, and articulating a comprehensive and pragmatic programme of activities aimed at progressively bringing about improvements. The recommendation arising from the Vienna Conference was that NHRAPs did not need to be binding but that they should have a strong persuasive character deriving from the process that leads to their creation.

Initial steps that might be identified as necessary in Ireland include:
- Coordinate disparate civil society actors into a broad-based human rights movement, including "traditional" human rights actors, media, churches and trade unions;
- Incorporate direct legal enforcement through a constitutional amendment to comply with existing treaty obligations;
- Strengthen the Human Rights Commission to become a catalyst promoting HRBA discussed in this document;
- Develop a national programme of human rights education and awareness-raising through formal and informal education, media debates, etc;

The above could lead to a process culminating in the adoption by 2010 of a National Human Rights Action Plan for the promotion and protection of human rights in Ireland's development.

The view of the UN Office of the High Commissioner for Human Rights in promoting NHRAPs is drawn on in the sections below. Since the adoption of the Vienna Declaration, there has emerged a rich body of experience of best practice in other countries – as well as lessons identified and available to inform a truly effective NHRAP in Ireland.

Australia was the first country to elaborate a NHRAP. This plan, covering the five-year period 1994-1998, was submitted to the UN Commission on Human Rights at its fiftieth session in early 1994. Since then plans have also been finalized by Bolivia, Brazil, Democratic Republic of the Congo, Ecuador, Indonesia, Latvia, Malawi, Mexico, Norway, the Philippines, South Africa, Sweden, Thailand, Venezuela and others.

The fundamental purpose of a NHRAP for Ireland would be to improve the promotion and protection of human rights in Ireland, by placing human rights improvements in the context of public policy. A NHRAP would require and facilitate Government and communities to endorse human rights improvements as practical goals, devise programmes to ensure the achievement of these goals, engage all relevant sectors of government and society, and allocate sufficient resources to its implementation.

> "The World Conference on Human Rights recommends that each State consider the desirability of drawing up a national action plan identifying steps whereby that State would improve the promotion and protection of human rights."
>
> **1993 Vienna Declaration and Programme of Action agreed by Ireland and 170 other states**

A young homeless man in the centre of Dublin.
© Cyril Byrne/Irish Times

The benefits of NHRAPs over ad hoc, less comprehensive approaches include:

- A national action plan should stimulate a more comprehensive assessment of needs in Ireland, by making plans explicit both to the Government itself and to the general public, thus generating a commitment that would not otherwise exist.
- National action plans are practical in orientation: they propose realistic activities, set achievable targets, ensure linkages with other national programmes and generate commitment to action.
- National action plans are a tool of sound public administration and governance, leading to stronger rule of law, enhancing management of the State and economic performance as well as human rights.
- A national action plan necessarily mobilizes a wide range of people and organizations in support of human rights activity. It therefore raises awareness and positive interest both within government and in the wider community.
- A comprehensive and structured approach is more likely to ensure that the concerns of specific or vulnerable groups, such as women, children and minorities are effectively addressed. Emphasising prevention, NHRAPs help develop programmes specifically directed towards addressing the human rights of vulnerable groups.
- National action planning takes an essentially non-confrontational approach to the consideration of human rights issues, acknowledging the legitimacy, without overstating the threat, of justiciability.

More specific purposes are:

- To provide guidance to government officials, NGOs, professional groups, educators, advocates and other members of civil society regarding the tasks that need to be accomplished to ensure that human rights are effectively observed and to promote co-operation among these groups.
- To strengthen the Irish Human Rights Commission and other issue-specific institutions dealing with human rights.
- To promote the universal ratification of international human rights treaties such as the Convention on the Protection of the Rights of All Migrant Workers and Members of Their Families.
- To facilitate the effective implementation of international standards and promote conformity of national legislation.
- To promote wider awareness of human rights standards and mechanisms, including among those whose actions are particularly critical, such as police, prison staff and politicians, as well as government officials and other workers in social fields.

The outcomes of a national action plan should include:

- Stronger legal frameworks based on international norms, more effective incorporation of human rights standards in domestic law, enhanced independence of the judiciary and more effective rule of law.
- Better protection for individuals and groups.
- A stronger culture of human rights.
- Stronger national institutions for the promotion and protection of human rights.
- More effective social programming to enhance the quality of life for all, particularly vulnerable groups, in areas such as education, health, housing, nutrition, social services and administration of justice.
- Improved national cohesion while respecting diversity.

A National Human Rights Action Plan requires considerable planning and resources. By its very nature it requires links to be made with existing national development frameworks and planning processes, e.g. in the areas of health, education, law enforcement and so forth. It is ultimately about ensuring that human rights concerns are not unwittingly quarantined as a separate "sector".

There is no defined time frame for a NHRAP, but the scale of what it requires to be effective suggests a period of approximately five years, specifically linking it to other relevant time frames. The key issue is to ensure that those involved have a deadline to structure their activities and to facilitate monitoring and final evaluation.

Central to an effective NHRAP is the concept of "ownership". A decision to embark on such a plan needs to be taken in the context of widespread, informed public debate. This requires:
- Informed political support;
- Transparent and participatory planning;
- Comprehensive baseline human rights study underlying the plan;
- Realistic prioritization and action-oriented planning;
- Clear success criteria and strong participatory mechanisms for monitoring and evaluation; and
- Adequate commitment of resources.

If these conditions are not in place, the danger is that a NHRAP is little more than a cosmetic exercise diminishing rather than enhancing human rights – adding to a growing mountain of other national plans.

11.3 General principles of NHRAPs

The OHCHR provides guidance to assist actors working on, or interested in, national human rights action plans, whether individuals, organizations representing government, parliamentarians, civil society, national human rights institutions, the judiciary or academics. It provides guidance on:
- The concept of NHRAP
- Institutional aspects
- Content and structure
- Development, implementation and monitoring
- International activity and experience

This section outlines the principles of NHRAPs under the following headings:

- NHRAP as a process as well as an outcome
- Commitment to universal human rights standards
- Implementing international human rights obligations
- Interdependence and indivisibility of human rights
- Action orientation
- NHRAP as a public document
- Monitoring and evaluation
- NHRAP as a continuing process
- NHRAP as a national undertaking
- The international dimension

"Our collective task is to find the means to turn international human rights commitments into reality, so that individual people and communities see a real difference in their lives. The challenges are many, and continue to defeat the best efforts of a whole range of national and international actors. To do its part to tackle them, OHCHR will pursue two overarching goals – protection and empowerment. Experience from many countries teaches us that human rights are most readily respected, protected and fulfilled when people are empowered to assert and claim their rights. Our work, therefore, should empower rights holders."

The OHCHR Plan Of Action: Protection And Empowerment 2003 **The United Nations High Commissioner For Human Rights**

A process as well as an outcome

A national action plan is both an outcome and a process, of equal importance. The outcome is the plan itself as well as each activity and change that flows from it. The plan should be developed as a significant and comprehensive document triggering activity across a wide range of areas of public administration. At the same time, the manner in which a national action plan is developed will influence its chances of success. Key elements are the extent to which the plan enjoys high-level support, the breadth and depth of the consultation process.

An elderly Traveller, living in appalling conditions in Tallaght
© *Pat Langan/Irish Times*

A national action plan must provide a central role for civil society. It should embrace the broadest range of participants from all sectors of society – human rights NGOs and community organizations of all types and private sector. The consultation process is crucial for the credibility and, ultimately, the effectiveness of the plan.

Consultation and coordination within Government are also crucial. The involvement of a wide range of government agencies in developing and implementing the plan will reinforce the notion that human rights are not just a matter for justice or foreign affairs ministries, but are the responsibility of Government as a whole. Commitment by public officials to the plan is vital to ensure that required human and financial resources are allocated.

Visible support from the top echelons of Government will help mobilize bureaucratic action and give a much higher public profile to the plan. Cross-party political support is also important. A NHRAP is part of a long-term process of enhancing national observance of universal standards that should survive changes of government and be above party political difference.

Commitment to universal human rights standards

A credible national action plan must be built on a commitment to Ireland's international legal obligations. These embrace both civil and political rights and economic, social and cultural rights. Ireland, together with the 170 other states attending the 1993 World Conference on Human Rights reaffirmed in the Vienna Declaration and Programme of Action "their commitment to the purposes and principles contained in the Charter of the United Nations and the Universal Declaration". Ireland reaffirmed "the solemn commitment of all States to fulfil their obligations to promote universal respect for, and observance and protection of, all human rights and fundamental freedoms for all" and stated that "the universal nature of these rights and freedoms is beyond question". A NHRAP must, as a minimum, conform to the standards set out in international human rights instruments.

Implementing international human rights obligations

Ireland's ratification of the various human rights treaties will only be truly effective when they are incorporated into Irish law. Policy and administrative steps will also be required to back up such ratification. In this process of giving practical effect to international obligations, a national action plan must review the range of Ireland's human rights commitments and propose steps to ensure that they are effectively observed.

Interdependence and indivisibility of human rights

Economic, social and cultural rights and civil/political rights are not inherently different. The right to health example, outlined above, highlights their interdependence and indivisibility as a practical issue. Similar analysis can be applied to most rights.

Action orientation

A national action plan must, of course, be action-oriented. Just as treaty ratification must be followed by steps to give effect to its content, so too the drafting of a national action plan must facilitate its implementation. Rather than setting forth claims and vague promises, a national action plan should:

- Indicate clearly the current human rights situation;
- Identify what problems need to be overcome;
- Specify what action will be taken (in terms that provide benchmarks for the evaluation of progress);
- Specify who is to take the action;
- Establish a time frame in which action will be taken; and
- Provide for effective monitoring and evaluation of, and accountability for, what has been done.

A public document

Dissemination: A national action plan is a public document that must be widely disseminated and accessible. The plan should be launched and reviewed with high-level political involvement to maximise media coverage. Alongside the plan, there should be a media strategy to ensure that the widest possible spectrum of the public is involved in the development and implementation of the plan. For this aspect of the plan to be implemented successfully, appropriate resources should be made available as an integral part of the plan.

Education: Implicit in the concept of a NHRAP is the central role of human rights education. A NHRAP can educate individuals as well as public officials about the human rights situation in their own country. Organizations or individuals responsible for specific aspects of the plan should be aware of the plan's requirements and given the necessary training or resources to enable them to meet the outcomes specified.

Tramore Pro-Refugee Group protest march.
© *Bryan O'Brien/Irish Times*

Translation and special needs: Where significant minority language groups exist, translation should be undertaken. Similarly, attention should be given to ensuring that citizens with special communication needs are taken into account, for example people with disabilities or poor literacy skills. A range of current initiatives regarding the Convention on the Rights of the Child, ECHR, etc., highlight how complex documents can be made accessible to even the youngest of children, etc.

Monitoring, evaluation and accountability

A NHRAP should incorporate mechanisms for monitoring progress and for evaluation of the plan's achievements and ensuring accountability. Human rights issues are an important area of public administration. Every effort should thus be made to avoid a situation in which human rights objectives are launched with great fanfare but are then left to wither because of lack of follow-through.

A variety of possible monitoring mechanisms exist but, whatever mechanism is chosen, it should have high-level support and credibility to ensure that its recommendations and proposals are acted upon. Monitoring should involve all relevant layers of Government in order to ensure that appropriate accountability is present to ensure the plan's implementation. Civil society as representatives of stakeholders should be a key part of the monitoring process. Any monitoring mechanisms should meet at reasonable intervals during the life of the plan and, towards the end of the life of the plan, an independent evaluation is desirable. The plan's achievements could then be assessed and recommendations made for subsequent plans.

A continuing process

Promoting and protecting human rights is a continuing process. There is no country that can expect to resolve all its human rights problems within a relatively short time frame. This means that a national human rights action plan should be viewed as part of a longer-term process. As one plan draws to an end, another should be developed to take its place. Subsequent plans should take into account emerging human rights issues, new international standards etc. The process of renewing a NHRAP should itself reinvigorate the commitment of all stakeholders to the promotion of human rights and enhance the dissemination of information about human rights.

A national undertaking

A NHRAP should be regarded as a truly national undertaking involving all elements of society. To make a real difference, it needs to be "owned" by the entire population.

The international dimension

An Irish NHRAP would be an unambiguous statement by the State domestically and to the outside world about its human rights agenda. A plan that reflects internationally agreed guidelines and accords with international best practice would not only facilitate Ireland in meeting its international obligations but would also lend credibility to efforts to advance its foreign policy objectives, enhance its prestige and promote human rights in other countries as a model for others wishing to take similar steps.

Endnotes

170. For instance, An Taoiseach, during Leaders' Questions in the Dáil on 9 February 2005, in the context for public demands for a right based Disability Bill, stated that the Bill published in 2004 was rights based, when the view of the Irish Human Rights Commission was that the Bill would satisfy neither the core minimum nor the progressive realisation of the rights of people with disabilities (*Observations on the Disability Bill* 2004). He further suggested that justiciable rights necessarily entail "some kind of rights based legislation that is lawyer-driven".

171. For example, a "rights based approach" based on national law is not necessarily consistent with a HRBA deriving from international human rights law. As such, a narrower "rights based approach" can serve to disempower and maintain the status quo.

172. As the State has rightly observed in its reports to various human rights treaty bodies, the incorporation of Ireland's human rights obligations by way of Constitutional amendment (as opposed to through legislation) is necessary for two reasons. Firstly, to ensure that the inadequacies of the Constitution's Directive Principles is remedied. Secondly, to ensure that socio-economic rights take precedence over any inconsistent legislation.

173. The Convention on the Protection of the Rights of All Migrant Workers and Members of Their Families is of particular importance given the dependence of Ireland on migrant labour for sustained economic growth; to facilitate the effective implementation of such standards and promote conformity of national legislation with international standards.

"A successful society is one where everyone is valued, has the opportunity to make the best of themselves and participate actively. It is a fair and just society. It is a society free from poverty – where there is equality and peace. It is a society where everyone has an adequate standard of living and access to good quality services. To what extent has Ireland been able to use its economic growth to build such a society?"

Combat Poverty Agency, *Annual Report 2003*

The debate regarding human rights in Ireland has to date taken place in an adversarial climate, with minimal public consultation and little informed political discussion. There has been even less discussion of human rights based approaches (HRBA) to Ireland's development.

A human rights based approach is a process, which applies a number of core principles aimed at ensuring the full enjoyment of human rights by all. It is based a number of core premises; Human rights are inherent to each and every one of us. They are set out in international human rights law, and states are legally bound to promote, protect and fulfil them. Human rights span all areas of life: civil activity, political freedom, social needs, economic well-being, cultural pursuits and environmental quality. Human rights based approaches should guide and direct, all state processes, under the five overarching principles of empowerment, participation, non-discrimination, accountability and the express application of international human rights law.

Much of the debate regarding human rights based approaches to Ireland's development has been monopolized by lawyers. While the issues and obligations involved are matters of law, a decision to use human rights as the litmus test for a State's success goes beyond questions of law – it signifies the kind of state, the kind of society, we choose to have.

"The core question here is as old as the first city states of Greece. It implicates a moral vision of the political community – of who is 'in' and who is 'out'. It concerns our societies' attitude towards human difference – whether this difference is one of race, creed or ability. It follows that the modern human rights agenda in the context of disability (and more generally) is not so much about power and protecting people against power (although that is very important in institutional settings) – it is about admitting people to power over their own lives and conferring on them equal rights to belong and to participate. It is about re-engineering social support to serve the overriding goal of expanding the zone of freedom to include all and not to maintain people – whether in misery or in luxury – on the periphery; squatting anxiously forever on the edge."[174]

Half a century after the UDHR was universally agreed and adopted on the international stage, with all the hopes and aspirations of that day, nations still strive to implement it. Though there certainly are examples of good practice and learning, no state has succeeded in truly taking human rights beyond rhetoric into practical reality. Ireland is no exception to this. Having signed to a whole array of international human rights law, it has not yet seen fit to fully respect and implement these binding obligations.

As it stands today, only a sub-category of the full spectrum of international human rights are protected in Ireland –mainly civil and political rights such as the right to a fair trial or the right to information. Economic, social and cultural rights are neither sufficiently recognised nor protected. Even at that, the checks and balances to ensure that these rights are protected are not always adequate. There are inherent contradictions in its approach, as the Government adopts laws, strategies and policies that are supposed to improve the protection of some rights, yet adopts other laws or polices that fundamentally undermine that purpose. Few policies, or strategies are human rights based and laws are not systematically human rights proofed.

The traditional position of successive Irish governments has been that economic, social and cultural rights are not "real" rights, and cannot or should not be afforded meaningful status in national law. The implication that rights, particularly economic, social and cultural rights, are a threat to the economy, is as misguided as it is incorrect. The untenable nature of this stance is evident in the Concluding Observations of treaty committees over the years and the subject of increasing challenges from NGOs, academics, and the Government's own human rights watchdog, the Irish Human Rights Commission.

The failure to address the root causes of disadvantage and social exclusion and to provide human rights based strategies and programmes has a number of grave consequences. There is a pervading sense of inequality of treatment by the State, a clientelist system of favours done for those with the necessary contacts or influence, evidenced by child poverty, rising homelessness, failure to significantly reduce the numbers of people admitted to mental health in-patient units, the poor material conditions in many primary schools, etc. While human rights based approaches prioritise the voice of the vulnerable and marginalised, they are no less relevant to the rest of society. There is increasing public frustration at political choices regarding expenditure of public resources, the failure to tackle the A&E crisis, social housing needs, etc. All too often these failures only surface when tribunals of enquiry investigate planning corruption, or the media exposes massive infrastructure overspend on projects such as roads. There is also rising unease at the growing gap between the "haves" and "have-nots". Yet, rarely are these issues recognised as human rights issues.

HRBA provide the vision, and importantly, also the method. HRBA are not merely reactive, where "victims" seek redress when their rights are violated, but rather they are proactive with 'rights holders' empowered to participate in shaping policy and building an equal and just society. HRBA force the State to demonstrate tangible results, i.e. actual and measurable improvements in health, housing, etc., and results that benefit all equally. Moreover, they provide the means to deliver real justice and equality. In essence they are about people having control over their lives. This process involves all groups in Irish society, at all levels. It spans from the empowerment and participation of society, to the ultimate accountability of those we have elected to power and all the agencies to which they delegate their functions.

Ireland's long-term future, and that of its children, will be shaped by the policies and programmes it sets now. These policies and programmes must be shaped by active and meaningful participation by all stakeholders, and rooted in the core human rights values, which all nations have agreed and developed over half a century. This is why a National Human Rights Action Plan, with which every plan, policy and strategy should be coherent, is recommended. Such a plan would provide a framework of core principles that would drive government activity, not just on society's behalf, but with the full and informed participation of society.

Ireland has committed itself before the international community to ensuring empowerment, participation, non-discrimination, accountability and the express application of international human rights law – the five components of human rights based approaches. Delivering these commitments requires vision, leadership, and commitment to long-term investment on the part of Government, and ownership of the process by the whole of society.

"Relative income poverty increased from 16% in 1994 to 20% in 1998 and 23% in 2003. This reflects increasing income inequality in Ireland and consequently the likelihood of a less socially cohesive society."

Combat Poverty Agency, *Ending Child Poverty: Policy Statement* **(2005)**

"[M]any people, especially young people, have little confidence in the political process. They are disillusioned because the political process fails to involve them in any real way, while also failing to address many of their core concerns. Transparency and accountability are demanded but rarely delivered. A new approach is clearly needed to address this issue."

CORI Justice Commission www.cori.ie/justice/soc_i ssues/participation.htm

Table 4: The National Human Rights Action Plan Process – OHCHR Handbook 2002

Preparatory Phase	Development	Implementation – Monitoring		Review
Consult within government	Frequent meetings of coordinating committee	Launch plan	Develop agreed reporting formats	Consider annual reports
Consult with NGOs and other interested groups	Conceptualize plan	Regular meetings of coordinating committee	Semi-annual assessments by coordinating committee	Appoint review panel
Appoint focal agency	Establish secretariat	Work with implementing partners		
	Establish sectoral working groups	Action by implementing agencies and partners	Input by civil society	Reports to Oireachtas & general public
Develop draft principles	Consult NGOs & other interested groups	Consultation and networking	Consultation and networking	
Government endorsement	Public meetings and public hearings	Media and dissemination strategy	Feedback to implementing agencies	Recommendations for successor plan
Public announcement	Prepare baseline study	Human rights education		
Organize initial meeting with interested groups	Identify priorities for special focus, vulnerable groups etc.	Legal status – endorsement by Oireachtas	Reports to parliament and general public	
Establish coordinating committee	Establish links with other national planning activities			
	Draft plan			
	Consider time frames			
	Consider legal status			

Annex 1: Resource bibliography and web links

Selected Resources on HRBA: Websites and other publications

The list below (supplementing those cited in the footnotes) includes materials selected on the basis of their assistance for policy review, training etc. They include a range of materials adaptable for different target groups, different sectors and to the Irish context. Inclusion does not imply endorsement of all contents. The list is supplemented by additional resources periodically updated at **www.ihrnetwork.org** and **www.amnesty.ie**

▓ **The UN Common Understanding on a Human Rights-Based Approach (HRBA) / HRBA to Programming in UNESCO: Perspectives from the Field**
http://portal.unesco.org/shs/en/ev.php-URL_ID=7914&URL_DO=DO_TOPIC&URL_SECTION=-465.html
Includes papers, field experience, power-point presentations, etc., based on UNESCOs training and steps to adopt HRBA.

▓ **The Human Rights Based Approach to Development Cooperation: Towards a Common Understanding Among the UN Agencies. Report of a UN Inter-agency workshop (May 2003)**
www.crin.org/docs/resources/publications/hrbap/HR_common_understanding.doc
This Statement of Common Understanding looks specifically at HRBA to development cooperation and development programming by UN agencies and their implications.

▓ **UNDP, Human Rights-Based Approach (HRBA) Checklist for Programme Staff**
http://hdr.undp.org/docs/network/hdr/thematics/HRBA_Checklist.pdf
A basic guide to the principles and treaties on human rights law, this manual also provides a practical 'to do' list for those hoping to implement a HRBA.

▓ **CARE, International, Basic Introduction to Human Rights and Rights-Based Programming**
www.careinternational.org.uk/resource_centre/civilsociety/basic_introduction_to_human_rights.pdf
This is a manual designed by a leading development NGO outlining a one-day workshop on HRBA. It provides both a facilitator's manual and material for participants.

▓ **Save The Children, Promoting Rights Based Approaches**
www.seapa.net/external/resources/crp.htm
This publication outlines an international NGO's experience in the HRBA programming.

▓ **Child Rights Information Network, Human Rights Based Programming Resources**
www.crin.org/hrbap/
This site provides a collection of key publications on rights-based programming.

▓ **Centre for Human Rights Education and Training**
www.erc.hrea.org
This website provides information about human rights education including presentations and training manuals, on-line and other human rights training from a variety of organizations.

▓ **Institute of International Education**
www.iie.org/ see "Publications" link for a range of publications including:

Dignity Counts: A guide to using budget analysis to advance human rights (2004):
A guide to using the budget as a tool to protect rights, particularly economic, social and cultural rights.

Circle of Rights—Economic, Social and Cultural Rights Activism:
A Training Resource (2000): Contains materials on specific rights, a rights-based approach, strategies and tools for economic, social and cultural (ESC) rights activism and suggested training methodologies for ESC rights training programs

Out of the Shadows (2000):
Educational video focusing on NGO work with respect to the UN Committee on Economic, Social and Cultural Rights,

A Rights-Based Approach to Budget Analysis (2000):
An introductory look at budget analysis as a tool for human rights activism.

Ripple in Still Water: Reflections by Activists on Local - and National – Level Work on Economic, Social and Cultural Rights (1997):
Introductory discussion of basic ESC rights concepts and work

AAAS Science and Human Rights Programme
http://shr.aaas.org/manuals/
Links to a range of manuals including:
Ahmed, Ferring, and Ibarra Ruiz, Manual on Environmental Health Indicators and Benchmarks: Human Rights Perspectives
Asher, **The Right to Health: A Resource Manual for NGOs**
Kunnemann & Epal-Ratjen, **The Right to Food: A Resource Manual for NGOs** Monitoring Labor Rights: A Resource Manual for NGOs

HURIDOCS
www.huridocs.org/othtools.htm
A range of tools including guides to monitoring human rights, advocacy using international mechanisms, etc.

DFID, Developing a Human Rights Based Approach to Addressing Maternal Mortality (2005)
www.dfid.gov.uk/pubs/files/maternal-desk.pdf

HIV/AIDS Stigma and Human Rights: A Resource Manual for NGOs, Community Groups and Persons Living with AIDS
www.humanrights.uio.no/forskning/programmer/sorafrika/Tswelopele%20manual.pdf
Training manual by Norwegian Centre for Human Rights aims to tackle stigma of HIV/AIDS at a local level. It is a practical tool introducing rights in an accessible format, with basic information on HIV/AIDS, why it is a human rights issue and common human rights issues for People Living with AIDS.

ODI, What Can We Do With A Rights-Based Approach To Development? (1999)
www.odi.org.uk/publications/briefing/3_99.html

■ VeneKlasen, et al, **Rights-based approaches and beyond: challenges of linking rights and participation**
www.ids.ac.uk/ids/bookshop/wp/wp235.pdf
IDS Working Paper 235 explores the growing trend of "rights-based approaches", drawing from interviews with a range of primarily US-based international human rights and development organizations.

■ Häusermann, **A Human Rights Approach to Development**
(Rights and Humanity/DFID 1998)
www.rightsandhumanity.org

■ Kenny, **Human Rights Based Development: Mapping with Dóchas Members**
IHRN review, carried out with Dóchas, the umbrella organisation for Irish development NGOs, identifying practical steps towards human rights based approaches in their development and humanitarian work.
www.ihrnetwork.org/hr-based-development.htm

■ Theis, **Promoting Rights-Based Approaches: Experiences and Ideas from Asia and the Pacific**
www.seapa.net/external/resources/promoting.zip
This collection outlines experience of HRBA in Asia, including a general overview of HRBA, experiences of different right-based organizations, practical suggestions, tools etc.

■ Hunt, Nowak and Osmani-OHCHR, **Draft Guidelines: A Human Rights Approach to Poverty Reduction Strategies** (2002)
www.unhchr.ch/development/povertyfinal.html
The Guidelines highlight the added value of HRBA to poverty reduction strategies.

■ **UNDP, Poverty Reduction and Human Rights** (2003)
www.undp.org/policy/docs/povertyreduction-humanrights0603.pdf
The Practice Note studies the integration of a HRBA into the current programme for development and Millennium Goals and outlines six concrete steps it will take to achieve these aims.

■ Nyamu-Musembi/Cornwall-Institute of Development Studies, **What is the Rights Based Approach All About? Perspectives from International Development Agencies** (2004)
www.grc-exchange.org/info_data/record.cfm?Id=1317&source=bulletin
and www.ids.ac.uk
This discussion paper analyses HRBA initiatives of international non-governmental organizations, multilateral and bilateral donors. Key issues explored include the transformative added value of HRBA and the implications for donors of adopting them.

■ Quinn, **Introductory Essay, From Charity to Rights – The Evolution of the Rights-Based Approach to Disability, International and Irish Perspectives** (2002)
www.accesswest.ie/intros/essayindex.html
This outlines human rights based approaches to disability from US, EU, Irish and International perspectives.

■ **OHCHR**, UN Guidelines for National Plans of Action for Human Rights Education (1997)
www.hrea.org/erc/Library/display.php?doc_id=211&category_id=21&category_type=3&group

The Guidelines have been developed by the OHCHR in the framework of the United Nations Decade for Human Rights Education (1995-2004) are intended to assist States seeking to develop national plans of action for human rights education.

▓ Report of Secretary-General UN, In Larger Freedom (2005)
www.un.org/largerfreedom
In September 2005, world leaders will come together at a summit in New York to review progress since the Millennium Declaration, adopted by all Member States in 2000. The goals of Freedom from Want, Freedom from Fear, Freedom from Dignity and Strengthening of the United Nations are considered in turn.

▓ International Network for Economic, Social and Cultural Rights
www.escr-net.org/EngGeneral/home.asp
The International Network for Economic, Social and Cultural Rights (ESCR-Net) is a collaborative initiative of groups and individuals from around the world working to secure economic and social justice through human rights. The website contains resources and learning programmes on ESC rights as well as information on events in the area of ESCR.

▓ UNDP
www.undp.org/governance/publications_full.htm#app
This website provides a range of resources relevant to HRBA in the context of the UNDP work, including:

> Details of UNDP work to apply a human rights-based approach to UNDP programming on Energy and Environmental programming, Poverty Reduction, Development in Uganda and HIV/AIDS
>
> Case studies and reports on Police Reform, Decentralization, NHRAPs
>
> Other Tools for Human Rights Based Programming, including Draft Guidelines and Terms of Reference for Human Rights Based Reviews of UNDP country programmes, Checklists, etc.
>
> Information about HURIST, including HURIST Status Report and Programme Document and analyses of the added value of a HRBA etc.

Annex 2: Glossary of Bodies

Constitutional Review Group (CRG)
The Constitutional Review Group was established by the Government of Ireland on the 27th April, 1995. Its job was to review the Constitution, and in light of this review, to establish those areas where constitutional change may be desirable or necessary. The Review Group published its report in 1996 and it is available from the Government Publications Office, Molesworth St., Dublin 2.

All-Party Oireachtas Committee on the Constitution
The All-Party Oireachtas Committee on the Constitution was established on the 17th December, 2002. The Committee is charged with completing a full review of the Constitution in order to establish those areas where change may be desirable or necessary. To date, the Committee has produced nine reports on various aspects of the Constitution and a tenth report, dealing with the Family, is expected in the near future.
See: www.oireachtas.ie/viewdoc.asp?fn=/documents/Committees29thDail/constitution.htm.

Economic and Social Research Institute (ESRI)

The ESRI's mission is to produce high-quality, independent research, relevant to Ireland's economic and social development, with the aim of informing policy-making and societal understanding. ESRI research has been a vital constituent of the national debate for over 40 years. Its in-depth analysis has underpinned many key national decisions, such as joining EMU, undertaking the National Development Plan and embarking on policies to combat poverty. See: www.esri.ie

National Economic and Social Council (NESC)

The National Economic and Social Council was established in 1973. The function of the Council is to analyse and report to the Taoiseach (Prime Minister) on strategic issues relating to the efficient development of the economy and the achievement of social justice and the development of a strategic framework for the conduct of relations and negotiation of agreements between the government and the social partners. The Council is chaired by the Secretary General of the Department of An Taoiseach and contains representatives of trade unions, employers, farmers' organizations, NGOs, key government departments and independent experts. See: www.nesc.ie

The UK Department for International Development (DFID)

The Department for International Development (DFID) is the part of the UK Government that manages Britain's aid to poor countries and works to alleviate extreme poverty. It was created in 1997 to replace the Overseas Development Agency (ODA) and is now headed by a Secretary of State with cabinet rank who is responsible to the UK Parliament for DFID. See: www.dfid.gov.uk

European Union (EU)

The European Union (EU) is a family of democratic European countries, committed to working together for peace and prosperity. Its Member States have set up common institutions to which they delegate some of their sovereignty so that decisions on specific matters of joint interest can be made democratically at European level. In the early years, much of the co-operation between EU countries related to trade and the economy, but now the EU also deals with many other subjects of direct importance for our everyday life, such as citizens' rights; ensuring freedom, security and justice; job creation; regional development; environmental protection; making globalisation work for everyone. See: europa.eu.int

Council of Europe (COE)

The Council of Europe is the continent's oldest political organisation, founded in 1949. It groups together 46 countries, including 21 countries from Central and Eastern Europe. The Council of Europe is distinct from the European Union. The Council's most significant achievement is the European Convention on Human Rights, which was adopted in 1950 and came into force in 1953. See: www.coe.int

European Convention on Human Rights and Fundamental Freedoms (ECHR)

The "European Convention on Human Rights" sets forth a number of fundamental rights and freedoms, such as the right to life, prohibition of torture, prohibition of slavery and forced labour. Parties undertake to secure these rights and freedoms to everyone within their jurisdiction. More rights are granted by additional protocols to the Convention. To ensure the observance of the obligations undertaken by the Parties, the European Court of Human Rights in Strasbourg has been set up. It deals with individual and inter-State petitions. See: www.coe.int

European Court of Human Rights

The European Court of Human Rights is the main enforcement machinery of the European Convention on Human Rights and Fundamental Freedoms, whereby states and individuals, regardless of their nationality, may refer alleged violations to the Court. Its jurisdiction is compulsory for all contracting parties. It sits on a permanent basis and is made up of judges from across the member states of the Council of Europe. The judges enjoy complete independence in the performance of their duties. See: www.echr.coe.int

European Social Charter

The European Social Charter sets out rights and freedoms and establishes a supervisory procedure guaranteeing their respect by the States Parties. All Europeans share these rights under the Charter and they affect every aspect of daily life, including housing, health, education, employment, legal and social protection, movement of persons and non-discrimination. See: www.coe.int/T/E/Human_Rights/Esc

Organisation for Security and Co-operation in Europe (OSCE)

With 55 States drawn from Europe, Central Asia and America, the OSCE is the world's largest regional security organization, bringing comprehensive and co-operative security to a region that stretches from Vancouver to Vladivostok. It offers a forum for political negotiations and decision-making in the fields of early warning, conflict prevention, crisis management and post-conflict rehabilitation, and puts the political will of the participating States into practice through its unique network of field missions. See: www.osce.org

Organisation of Economic Co-operation and Development (OECD)

The OECD groups 30 member countries sharing a commitment to democratic government and the market economy. It has active relationships with some 70 other countries, NGOs and civil society. Best known for its publications and its statistics, its work covers economic and social issues from macroeconomics, to trade, education, development and science and innovation. See: www.oecd.org

The United Nations (UN)

The United Nations (UN), which emerged in 1945 from the devastation of global conflict, aims to "save succeeding generations from the scourge of war". Its mission is to maintain international peace and security and to promote friendly relations between countries. The UN Charter upholds human rights and proposes that states should work together to overcome social, economic, humanitarian and cultural challenges. See: www.un.org

United Nations High Commissioner for Refugees (UNHCR)

The Office of the United Nations High Commissioner for Refugees was established on December 14, 1950 by the United Nations General Assembly. The agency is mandated to lead and coordinate international action to protect refugees and resolve refugee problems worldwide. Its primary purpose is to safeguard the rights and well-being of refugees. It strives to ensure that everyone can exercise the right to seek asylum and find safe refuge in another State, with the option to return home voluntarily, integrate locally or to resettle in a third country. See www.unhcr.org

United Nations Office of the High Commissioner for Human Rights (OHCHR)

The United Nations vision is of a world in which the human rights of all are fully respected and enjoyed in conditions of global peace. The High Commissioner works to keep that vision to the forefront through constant encouragement of the international community and its member States to uphold universally agreed human rights standards. In addition it is the role of the OHCHR to be a voice for the victims of human rights violations everywhere. See: www.ohchr.org

United Nations Commission on Human Rights
The United Nations Commission on Human Rights meets each year in March/April for six weeks in Geneva. Over 3,000 delegates from Governments and from non-governmental organizations participate. During its regular annual session, the Commission adopts about a hundred resolutions, decisions and Chairperson's statements on matters of relevance to the human rights of individuals in all regions and circumstances. It is assisted in this work by the Sub-Commission on the Promotion and Protection of Human Rights, a number of working groups and a network of individual experts, representatives and rapporteurs mandated to report to it on specific issues. See: www.unhchr.ch/html/menu2/2/chr.htm

United Nations Economic and Social Council (ECOSOC)
The council spearheads the UN's economic, social, humanitarian and cultural activities. It oversees the work of a number of commissions which deal with human rights, population growth, technology and drugs, among other issues. See: www.un.org/docs/ecosoc

United Nations Committee on Economic, Social and Cultural Rights
The primary function of the Committee is to monitor the implementation of the International Covenant on Economic, Social and Cultural Rights by State parties. It strives to develop a constructive dialogue with State parties and seeks to determine through a variety of means whether or not the norms contained in the Covenant are being adequately applied and how the implementation and enforcement of the Covenant could be improved so that all people who are entitled to the rights enshrined in the Covenant can actually enjoy them in full. See: www.ohchr.org/english/bodies/cescr

United Nations Children's Fund (UNICEF)
The United Nations International Children's Emergency Fund (UNICEF) was established by the United Nations General Assembly in 1946. In 1953, its name was shortened to the United Nations Children's Fund, but is still known by its popular acronym. Headquartered in New York City, UNICEF provides long-term humanitarian and developmental assistance to children and mothers in developing countries. A voluntarily funded agency, UNICEF relies on contributions from governments and private donors. Its programmes emphasize developing community-level services to promote the health and well-being of children. UNICEF was awarded the Nobel Peace Prize in 1965. See: www.unicef.org

United Nations Development Programme (UNDP)
UNDP is the UN's global development network, an organization advocating for change and connecting countries to knowledge, experience and resources to help people build a better life. UNDP is on the ground in 166 countries, working with them on their own solutions to global and national development challenges. UNDP also helps developing countries attract and use aid effectively. In all their activities, UNDP encourages the protection of human rights and the empowerment of women. See: www.undp.org

The Human Rights Strengthening Programme (HURIST)
A joint UNDP-OHCHR programme which works to support national governments in their

development planning by developing methodologies and identifying best practices in HRBA. See: www.undp.org/governance/hurist.htm

International Labour Organisation (ILO)

The International Labour Organization is the United Nations specialized agency which seeks the promotion of social justice and internationally recognized human and labour rights. It was founded in 1919 and is the only surviving major creation of the Treaty of Versailles which brought the League of Nations into being and it became the first specialised agency of the UN in 1946. The ILO formulates international labour standards in the form of Conventions and Recommendations setting minimum standards of basic labour rights. Within the UN system, the ILO has a unique tripartite structure with workers and employers participating as equal partners with governments in the work of its governing organs. See: www.ilo.org

The World Health Organisation (WHO)

The World Health Organization is the United Nations specialized agency for health. It was established on 7 April 1948. WHO's objective is the attainment by all peoples of the highest possible level of health. Health is defined as a state of complete physical, mental and social well-being and not merely the absence of disease or infirmity. See: www.who.org

The World Bank

The World Bank is a United Nations' specialized agency, and it's mission is to fight poverty and improve the living standards of people in the developing world. It is a development Bank which provides loans, policy advice, technical assistance and knowledge sharing services to low and middle income countries to reduce poverty. See: www.worldbank.com

International Monetary Fund (IMF)

The IMF is an international organization of 184 member countries. It was established to promote international monetary co-operation, exchange stability, and orderly exchange arrangements; to foster economic growth and high levels of employment; and to provide temporary financial assistance to countries to help ease balance of payments adjustment. See: www.imf.org

Annex 3: NGO Profiles

www.trocaire.org

1 Name, date of establishment and website of your organization.
Trócaire was established in 1973.

2. Principle objectives, areas of work, activities, target group, etc.
Trócaire has a dual mandate: 1. to support long-term development programmes overseas and provide emergency relief; 2. at home to inform the Irish public about the root causes of poverty and injustice and be an effective advocate for justice at the national and international level. Its overseas work includes interventions and partners in 55 developing countries on themes such as livelihood security, development of civil society, peace building & conflict transformation, HIV/AIDS and emergency, recovery and disaster prevention.

From its foundation, Trócaire's mandate stressed that the developed world's duties to the developing countries is "no longer a matter of charity, but of simple justice". It adopts a development rights analysis, interpreting human rights to cover political, civil, economic, social, cultural and collective rights.

3. Reasons why your organization seeks to embrace human rights based approaches in its work.

Trócaire's analysis of the root causes of poverty focuses on issues of inequality, injustice and power imbalances. Trócaire sees the violation of Civil, Political, Economic, Social and Cultural rights and the denial of the right to Development and the right to participate as root causes of marginalisation and poverty. The necessity of HRBA is also highlighted by audits of its overseas projects and consultations with partners which confirm that much of Trócaire's work is either the result of failure of participation (leading to and perpetuating conflict, human rights abuses, etc.) or aims to be a catalyst for participation. Trócaire sees the right to participate as the entry point for realising all the other rights. Trócaire's Strategic Plan seeks to mainstream human rights in all its programme sectors (HIV/AIDS, Livelihood Security, Peace Building & Conflict Transformation, Development of Civil Society) and in the organization's response to emergencies.

4. How do you apply this commitment in practice?

Partnership with civil society organizations in the South is a core value and also the key approach to development and emergency programming. Trócaire advances human rights based approaches by a variety of means. In its overseas work, Trócaire supports initiatives that strengthen the ability of individuals and groups in developing countries to claim their rights, hold the state accountable for its obligations and participate in decisions that affect their lives. Indeed, the development of civil society for Trócaire is key to address power imbalances, ensure respect of human rights and support processes that will make the state, the market and indeed civil society organizations themselves more accountable to people. In Ireland and internationally, Trócaire uses policy and advocacy work to change the structures, systems and policies that deny rights. Key policy areas include PRSP, trade and UN Millennium Development Goals.

Trócaire is also engaged in development education with young people in Ireland and works to mobilise mass support to campaign for the rights of poor countries and people, such as the Make Poverty History campaign. Human rights awareness is also a key element of its fundraising and communication work.

5. Challenges faced by your organization in adopting and implementing HRBA.

HRBA is enshrined in Trócaire's mission and philosophy. At an operational level, the fact that Trócaire works in partnership with civil society organizations in developing countries presents both opportunities and challenges. Partnering local groups and strengthening the fabric of civil society represent the best strategy to ensuring respect for rights in a very practical and culturally sensitive way. However, some partners adopt a "service delivery" (as opposed to a "human rights based") approach to their work. The challenge for Trócaire is to accompany them in the transition from service delivery to rights based work; and to provide training and technical support as required. To familiarise Trócaire with rights language and practical rights approaches, further integrating HRBA into our work, training is key. In addition, as our work overseas has been primarily project based, opportunities to link the micro with the macro and to strengthen the rights and advocacy dimension of our programme work have not been realised to the full. This is being addressed by introducing systems and policies that will facilitate a shift from the project model to the programmatic approach informed by a HRBA perspective.

6. Success or added value which you attribute to applying HRBA.

Trócaire sees the full realisation of human rights as the ultimate aim of development. Technical solutions are not enough to eradicate poverty and bring about a fair and just world. The application of HRBA and the identification, in particular, of the right to participate has facilitated the adoption of a greater focus on linking the micro with the macro and integrating programme and advocacy work. In Trócaire's experience, only a human rights based approach to development will ensure that the structural causes of poverty and injustice are identified and addressed. Overseas, the application of HRBA to mobilise people strengthens all levels of democratic and social structures. This in turn is key to improve political life, ensure accountable governance and respect for human rights. In Ireland, Trócaire's education and campaign work facilitates the evolution of constituencies which actively work to change structures and policies which perpetuate social injustice and poverty.

7. Future plans to develop your organization's HRBA.

Human rights are at the core of Trócaire's mission and philosophy. Ongoing efforts by Trócaire to further develop HRBA in its work include: research and analysis of its work from a rights perspective; integration of the human rights discourse in its Strategic Plan and thematic policies; participation in debates and fora seeking to define and operationalise rights based approaches; increase understanding and expertise of rights based approaches among programme staff and partners.

Simon Communities of Ireland
www.simoncommunity.com

1 Name, date of establishment and website of your organization.

Simon Communities of Ireland was established in Ireland in 1969

2. Principle objectives, areas of work, activities, target group, etc.

The Simon Communities of Ireland is the federation of seven Simon Communities in the Republic of Ireland: Cork, Dublin, Dundalk, Galway, Midlands, North West and South East. Simon provides a range of services to people who are homeless, including street outreach, emergency services, settlement support and long-term housing. We are committed to the elimination of homelessness in Ireland and to using our expertise as a service provider to progress solutions with our statutory and non-statutory partners.

3. Reasons why your organisation seeks to embrace human rights based approaches in its work.

Pursuing a constitutional and legislative right to housing has been a policy commitment of the organisation for over 20 years. In recent years – through the resourcing of the post of Social Policy and Research Coordinator this has gained new impetus. We were conscious of a potential paradox of campaigning for a political agenda which we may not ourselves be delivering in our projects, our fundraising and our advocacy work.

4. How do you apply this commitment in practice?

At a policy level we have engaged with both domestic and international law and instruments to progress our agenda including: a full review of the 1988 Housing Act, promotion of the rights agenda in the National Anti-Poverty Strategy, cross border lobbying and policy submissions on the Good Friday Agreement, publicising the UN Committee on Economic, Social and Cultural Rights' comments on Ireland. We are now beginning to mainstream human rights as a framework for delivering our services through the strategic plan for the entire federation and through individual community plans. This will necessitate training for staff and volunteers and advocacy with and for service users.

5. Challenges faced by your organisation in adopting and implementing HRBA.

Finding the time and space to engage people with the agenda, and imagining what HRBA will practically mean, reassuring ourselves that it is a re-orientation of our work rather than a re-invention.

6. Success or added value which you attribute to applying HRBA.

Long-term, we think we will empower our service users and re-invigorate our staff, while adding credibility and cross-organizational cohesiveness to our campaigning agenda.

7. Future plans to develop your organization's HRBA.

Amnesty / Simon training, "Delivering Homeless Services in a Human Rights Context", being mainstreamed. Specific training with service users in autumn of 2005. Conference early in 2006 pulling together learning thus far. Increased campaigning on and mainstreaming of HRBA under new strategy.

Pavee Point Travellers Centre

www.paveepoint.ie

1. Name, date of establishment and website of your organization.

Pavee Point Travellers Centre was founded in January 1985.

2. Principle objectives, areas of work, activities, target group, etc.

Pavee Point's work is based on two key premises: real improvement in Travellers' living circumstances and social situation requires the active involvement of Travellers themselves; and non-Travellers have a responsibility to address the various processes which serve to exclude Travellers from participating as equals in society. The key values which inform the work of the organization are: human rights; social solidarity; cultural diversity; community development; multi-dimensionality; partnership; and equality. Key areas of work include: community development; education; economic development; health; culture and heritage; mediation; youth work; drugs; and violence against women.

3. Reasons why your organization seeks to embrace human rights based approaches in its work.

Pavee Point believes that all peoples have rights which also involve duties and responsibilities. Therefore members of the majority population have a responsibility to become involved in supporting minorities to achieve their rights. Pavee Point believes that all people should have access to resources which enable them to meet basic human needs, to reach a socially acceptable standard of living and to live with dignity in society. Furthermore women's rights and cultural rights are indivisible from other human rights. Pavee Point maintains that Travellers should be able to realise their potential as equal citizens and contribute to the development of society. Pavee Point believes in Travellers' right to self-determination by being key agents in their own development for the future and by developing internal solidarity within the Traveller community.

4. How do you apply this commitment in practice?

Pavee Point has made submissions and lobbied on a range of UN treaties including CERD, ICESCR, ICCPR, CEDAW and CRC, and the Council of Europe Framework Convention for the Protection of National Minorities; and on the incorporation of the ECHR into Irish law. With regard to domestic legislation Pavee Point has made submissions and lobbied on the Prohibition of Incitement to Hatred Act and equality legislation; and on issues such as accommodation. A Traveller member of staff is a member of the Irish Human Rights Commission. In-service training takes place to ensure that staff members and programme participants have an opportunity to discuss human rights issues and how they should be addressed in a manner that is relevant to Travellers.

5. Challenges faced by your organization in adopting and implementing HRBA.

Solidarity is a key principle within the organization but it has been challenging at times to encourage all members of the organization to see the value of working on issues that they may have no direct interest in or feel engaging in such issues represents a cultural clash for them. The depth of the exclusion facing Travellers is such that many members of the community feel little or no progress can ever be made, pursuing a human rights approach demands a lot of human resources and commitment - these dynamics can pull against each other and make already challenging work even more so.

6. Success or added value which you attribute to applying HRBA.

HBRA provide a framework through which to articulate the issues facing the Traveller community: it facilitated a movement away from a services provider / social work approach to working on Travellers' issues and created the conditions for an approach that sees Travellers as key actors in the pursuit of their own rights. In parallel with this, the range of international instruments Ireland has signed up to provides a marker against which to measure success or otherwise of the work on Traveller human right's issues and an opportunity to raise the bar on how these issues should be addressed.

7. Future plans to develop your organization's HRBA.

Human rights have been an integral part of Pavee Point's approach to its work and will continue to be so.

Endnotes

174. Professor Gerard Quinn, (now Member of Irish Human Rights Commission), addressing 4th Annual Department of Foreign Affairs NGO Human Rights Forum, Dublin, July 2001.